# Mannequins in M

*Mannequins in Museums* is a collection of historical and contemporary case studies that examine how mannequins are presented in exhibitions and shows that, as objects used for storytelling, they are not neutral objects.

Demonstrating that mannequins have long histories of being used to promote colonialism, consumerism, and racism, the book shows how these histories inform their use. It also engages readers in a conversation about how historical narratives are expressed in museums through mannequins as surrogate forms. Written by a select group of curators and art historians, the volume provides insight into a variety of museum contexts, including art, history, fashion, anthropology, and wax. Drawing on exhibition case studies from North America, South Africa, and Europe, each chapter discusses the pedagogical and aesthetic stakes involved in representing racial difference and cultural history through mannequins. As a whole, the book will assist readers to understand the history of mannequins and their contemporary use as culturally relevant objects.

*Mannequins in Museums* will be compelling reading for academics and students in the fields of museum studies, art history, public history, anthropology, and visual and cultural studies. It should also be essential reading for museum professionals who are interested in rethinking mannequin display techniques.

**Bridget R. Cooks** is Associate Professor in the Department of Art History and the Department of African American Studies at the University of California, Irvine, and Associate Director of the Institute and Museum of California Art. Her research focuses on African American artists, Black visual culture, and museum criticism. Cooks has worked as a museum educator and curator for several exhibitions. She is author of the book *Exhibiting Blackness: African Americans and the American Art Museum* (University of Massachusetts Press, 2011). Some of her other publications can be found in *Afterall*, *Afterimage*, *American Studies*, *Aperture*, and

*American Quarterly*. She is currently completing her next book, *Norman Rockwell: The Civil Rights Paintings*.

**Jennifer J. Wagelie** is Academic Liaison at the Jan Shrem and Maria Manetti Shrem Museum of Art at the University of California, Davis. She received her PhD in art history from the Graduate Center, City University of New York. Her area of study is the art of the Pacific Islands, specifically Māori art and material culture, with other research interests in the history of museums, collections, and exhibitions. She has worked at the National Gallery of Art, Washington DC and the Sidney and Lois Eskenazi Museum of Art, Indiana University and taught at University of California, Santa Cruz and California State University, Sacramento. She has also held postdoctoral fellowships in the anthropology departments of the University of British Columbia, Vancouver and the Smithsonian Institution's National Museum of Natural History.

# Mannequins in Museums

## Power and Resistance on Display

Edited by Bridget R. Cooks and Jennifer J. Wagelie

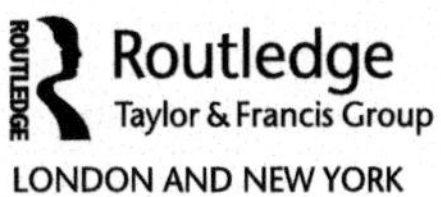

LONDON AND NEW YORK

First published 2022
by Routledge
2 Park Square, Milton Park, Abingdon, Oxon OX14 4RN

and by Routledge
605 Third Avenue, New York, NY 10158

*Routledge is an imprint of the Taylor & Francis Group, an informa business*



*British Library Cataloguing-in-Publication Data*
A catalogue record for this book is available from the British Library

*Library of Congress Cataloging-in-Publication Data*
Names: Cooks, Bridget R., 1972– editor. | Wagelie, Jennifer J., editor.
Title: Mannequins in museums : power and resistance on display / edited by Bridget R. Cooks and Jennifer J. Wagelie.
Description: London ; New York : Routledge, Taylor & Francis Group, 2022. | Includes bibliographical references and index.
Identifiers: LCCN 2021015421 (print) | LCCN 2021015422 (ebook) | ISBN 9780367202682 (hardback) | ISBN 9781032036168 (paperback) | ISBN 9780429260575 (ebook)
Subjects: LCSH: Museum manikins. | Museums and minorities. | Art—Exhibitions—Social aspects. | Art—Exhibitions—Philosophy.
Classification: LCC AM151 .M314 2022 (print) | LCC AM151 (ebook) | DDC 069/.5—dc23
LC record available at https://lccn.loc.gov/2021015421
LC ebook record available at https://lccn.loc.gov/2021015422

ISBN: 978-0-367-20268-2 (hbk)
ISBN: 978-1-032-03616-8 (pbk)
ISBN: 978-0-429-26057-5 (ebk)

DOI: 10.4324/9780429260575

Typeset in Times New Roman
by Apex CoVantage, LLC

# Contents

# Figures

# Contributors

**Bridget R. Cooks** is Associate Professor in the Department of Art History and the Department of African American Studies at the University of California, Irvine.

**Gwyneira Isaac** is Curator of North American Ethnology in the Department of Anthropology at the National Museum of Natural History, Smithsonian Institution, Washington, DC.

**Lanisa S. Kitchiner** is Chief of the African and Middle Eastern Division at the Library of Congress, Washington, DC.

**Emma McClendon** is a fashion historian, curator, and author based in New York City.

**Kyunghee Pyun** is Associate Professor of art history at the Fashion Institute of Technology, New York.

**Minou Schraven** teaches art history and museum studies at Amsterdam University College and is a research fellow at the Amsterdam Centre for Religious History, Vrije Universiteit Amsterdam.

**Jessica Stephenson** is Associate Professor of Art History at Kennesaw State University, Georgia.

**Jennifer J. Wagelie** is Academic Liaison at the Jan Shrem and Maria Manetti Shrem Museum of Art at the University of California, Davis.

# Acknowledgments

Many individuals and experiences have contributed to the development of this volume. We appreciate the College Art Association for including our panel “The ‘Man’ in Mannequin: Humankind on Display” in its 2011 conference that served as the platform for creating *Mannequins in Museums*. We are thankful for the critical engagement of the authors featured here, several of whom presented in the conference session. We are indebted to the vision, professionalism, and support of Heidi Lowther, Editor of the Museum & Heritage Studies and Library & Information Science series, and Kangan Gupta, Editorial Assistant of Anthropology, Archaeology, and Museum and Heritage Studies at Routledge Books. Thanks to Robert G. Moeller for his editorial advice and interest in this scholarship. All of the chapters benefitted from a variety of experts, including anthropologists, archaeologists, artists, curators, designers, and museum staff at the institutions discussed in our texts. We appreciate the generosity they have shown the contributors. Special thanks to Dr. JoAnne Martin, co-founder of the National Great Blacks in Wax Museum, Thomas Dolby, and Kathleen Beller for making the experience of the museum truly exceptional.

We would like to thank each other for the countless funny and critical conversations we have had over the years about our shared fascination with mannequins. Childhood experiences of Great Moments with Mr. Lincoln at Disneyland, natural history museums, and department store window displays sparked our curiosity about the history of mannequins in museums that ultimately led us to this project. How lucky are we to have met as interns at the National Gallery of Art in 1997 and stayed friends and colleagues for all of these years.

Finally, we would like to thank our families, particularly Harvey and Joe, for their unwavering support for all of our good ideas and discouragement of the bad ones.

# Introduction

*Bridget R. Cooks and Jennifer J. Wagelie*

Mannequins function as storytelling objects in museums. Although they may appear to be objective, and perhaps even neutral objects used to present historic costumes, exact physiognomic details, or to bring the past to life, mannequins, like the bodies they represent, have origins and histories. They are "born" from a complex context of decisions made by individuals with particular perspectives and agendas. Studying these decisions and their impact on museum viewers can tell us at least as much as the mannequin displays themselves. *Mannequins and Museums: Power and Resistance on Display* is a collection of historical and contemporary case studies written by authors who examine how mannequins function. Although mannequins are used widely in museums of different kinds, much of their role in the "exhibitionary complex" of museums remains to be critically considered.[1] This book seeks to change that by discussing the pedagogical and aesthetic stakes involved in representing racial differences and cultural history through mannequins.

We define mannequins as forensic reconstructions of human remains, fashion mannequins and dress forms, customized life-size figurative forms, and cast figures made from composite materials including wax, plaster, and plastics. As an illustrative part of museum exhibitions, mannequins are devices for teaching viewers about "other" people from nations and time periods different from their own. Mannequins also serve as perfected examples of human forms in size, shape, and color that idealize types of beauty. Their function as model humans has consequences for how viewers assess humanity over time. Mannequins can, at worst, fix racial differences in an antiquated mode of polygenesis, or better, situate viewers within an embodied ancestral legacy informed though the presence of a simulated identity. As a whole, this volume forms a basis for exploring the practical application and affective power of mannequins as proxies for humans in a variety of museum contexts including anthropology, art, fashion, history, and wax. In

DOI: 10.4324/9780429260575-I

doing so, the authors demonstrate that the use of mannequins in museums plays a role in the institutional "articulation of power and knowledge."[2]

As surrogates for human bodies, mannequins are tools for economic consumerism and instruction. For example, in retail windows mannequins are aspirational forms used to cultivate viewer's desires. In this context, viewers are invited to replace the mannequins by becoming wearers of the garments presented. In some museum exhibitions, mannequins' hyper-realistic features support the authority of the museum through the appearance of objective authenticity. In other exhibitions, mannequins function as human placeholders without articulated features that would suggest race or nationality. Instead, through incomplete bodies, they exist as incomplete gestures toward the human. In the living world, the generic body does not exist. However, within the contexts of museums, mannequins are presented with a security of a normative identity in scenarios that stop time and create a moment for spectacular viewing.

Positioned in a narrative tableau, mannequins can lend a reality effect to a museum's attempt to tell a historical truth. By creating a phenomenological encounter with the viewer, mannequins become conduits for telling stories in a manner that curators think *should* be told, for better or worse. Because of this, mannequins have long histories in the promotion of colonialism, consumerism, sizeism, and racism that inform their use. At the turn of the twentieth century, didactic life-groups on display in the Anthropology Hall in the United States National Museum (now the National Museum of Natural History, Smithsonian Institution (NMNH) showed Asian, Native American, and Pacific mannequins performing daily rituals in rows of airless glass boxes. The dioramas objectified people and their cultures into a pre-modern past that justified their disappearance from a living present and active future.[3] By the 1960s, the use of mannequins, or their more anthropological term, "manikins," featured prominently in the redesigned Pacific Island installations at both the Smithsonian and the Field Museum of Chicago. Of particular note was the Field Museum's inclusion of a multigenerational Māori "nuclear family," that was sealed inside the institution's Māori meetinghouse constructing a manufactured view of domesticity in an attempt to make a culturally distant people more relatable to Midwestern museum visitors, but only exoticized their differences.[4]

More recently, in what has been called the "unanticipated session" at the American Alliance of Museums Annual Meeting in 2017, the LF Creative Group presented a mannequin display of an enslaved African man standing on a wooden platform, chained and tied to a post beside his White auctioneer whose skin and clothes were depicted in shades of gray. This dramatic and disturbing scene was selected for exhibition in order to advertise the company's offerings to museums.[5] Responses to the display by conference

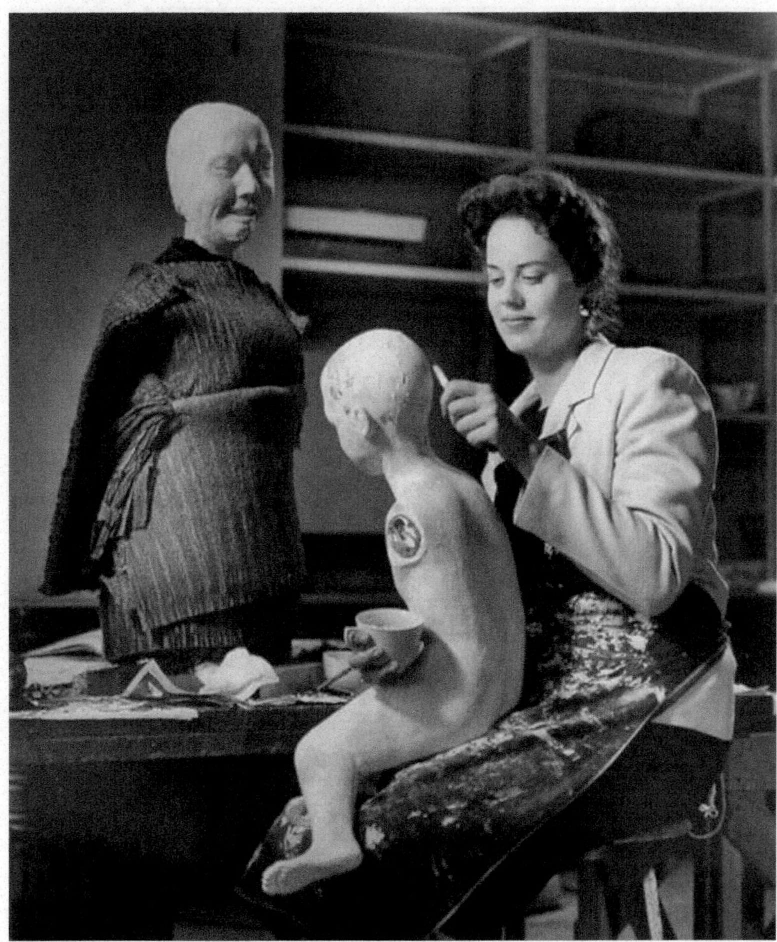

*Figure 0.1* Photograph of preparator Susan Schanck carving Māori manikins.

*Source:* © The Field Museum, Image No. A98324.

attendees quickly spawned postings in the Twitterverse with the hashtag #2017SlaveAuction with comments such as: "Too long a history of museums making dioramas out of the pain and humiliation of people of color. No thank you"; "Us addressing #AAM2017Slave Auction not about artistic expression or freedom of speech, about upholding museum values, inform/educ the public"; and "What kind of relationship do museums envision themselves creating with Black visitors via this kind of representation?"[6]

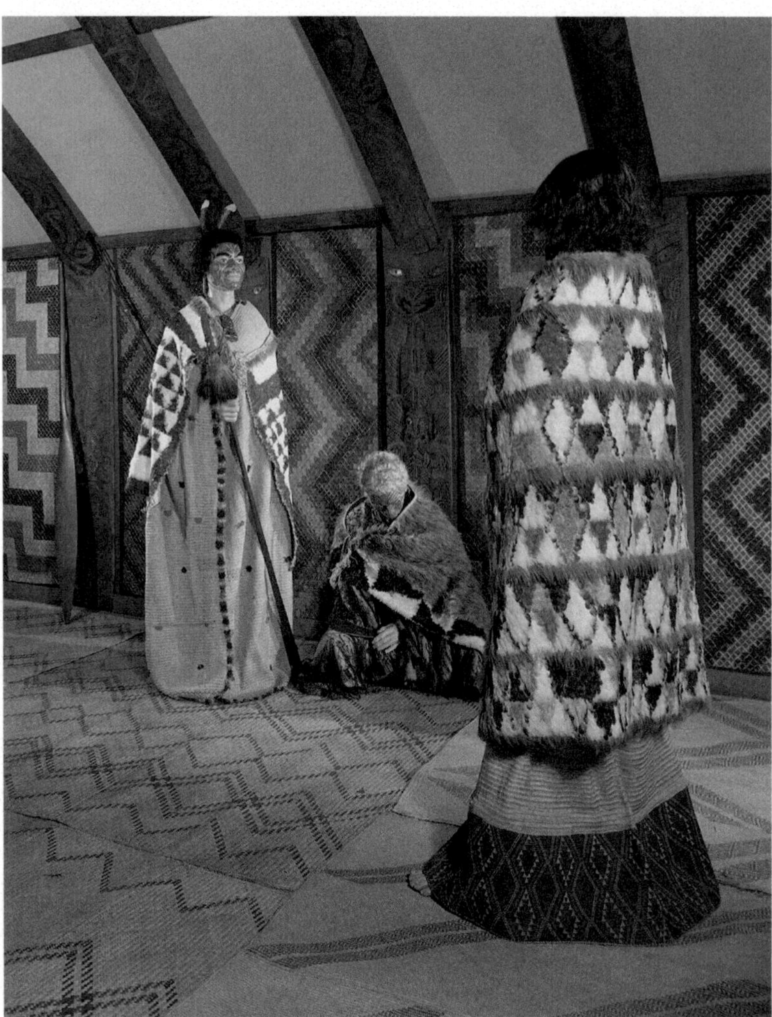

*Figure 0.2* Photograph of manikins inside *Ruatepupuke* at the Field Museum, Chicago, 1962.

*Source:* © The Field Museum, Image No. A98327.

Over 100 people joined the impromptu meeting session with representatives from the LF Creative Group to discuss the makers' intentions and viewers' responses.[7] The custom-made fabricators' display of a potential museum encounter focused viewers on the significance of mannequins as objects that can relay cultural values. The museum professionals at the annual meeting seized the retail opportunity to create a moment for conversation and ultimately, intervention. By thinking critically about the use of mannequins through moments of public engagement, this book aims to invite curators, educators, historians, students, and exhibition viewers in a conversation about how mannequins aid in museums' expressions of social and cultural narratives.

Because anxieties around nationalism, empire, and antiquated myths of racial hierarchies circulate today with fervor, the perception of our pasts still matters. While the subject of mannequins has been relatively scant in scholarly circles, there are numerous examples of events in recent popular culture that have brought mannequins into contemporary discourse. The 2013 invention by Swiss-based manufacturers, Pro Infirmis, of mannequins that feature physical deformations and visible disabilities;[8] public criticism of department store clothing mannequins with pronounced ribs and collarbones;[9] the 2018 decommission of the mannequins in the "bride auction" staged in the Pirates of the Caribbean ride at Disneyland;[10] and the popular live life-group fad #MannequinChallenge of 2016 when subjects would stand motionless in a tableau vivant for short videos to imitate dioramas, all point toward the scope of mannequins in daily visual culture through consumerism and entertainment. This last example, performed by figures as famous as First Lady Michelle Obama, superstar athlete LeBron James, and musician Sir Paul McCartney, #MannequinChallenge reminded viewers of the public fascination with mannequins in museums, while demonstrating a curious and possibly latent longing to become a museum display and fulfill a desire for immortality.[11]

Existing books on the topic of mannequins mainly focus on their role in the fashion industry. Twentieth century innovator, Ralph Pucci, has earned attention for his defining influence in mannequin style and design.[12] Other literature discusses the role of mannequins as props to heighten successful department store sales in the nineteenth and twentieth centuries.[13] Various publications mention artists' use of mannequins from the nineteenth century until now as stand-ins for live models and as components in contemporary practices for artists such as Yinka Shonibare and Fred Wilson.[14] Most relevant to this book is *Living Pictures, Missing Persons: Mannequins, Museums, and Modernity* by Mark B. Sandberg. In his text, Sandberg uses the term "effigy" to describe the physical presence of mannequins in Western European visual culture, as well as their absences. He argues that effigies in the period from about 1880 to 1920 enabled mobilization and relocation in a modern age of dislocation, disorientation, and technological invention. Mannequins played their part in the delivery of immersive mimetic experiences along with advances in cinema and photography. Specifically, in the context of Scandinavian folk museums, mannequins made memories of the rural past accessible to urban visitors across class, industrial, and temporal changes. The importance of this discussion is less about the mannequins as objects, and more about the sites of struggle they embody. Addressing the issues at stake in the use of mannequins helps viewers think through the visual to the more abstract yet pervasive concerns of personal and symbolic identities.

It is for all of these reasons that now is the time to examine the role of museums – receptacles and generators of cultural life – in shaping the perception and interpretation of cultural differences. The authors in *Mannequins in Museums* clarify the stakes of cultural representation in exhibitions by offering an informed account of the state of the field. Each chapter provides an insider's perspective into how mannequins are made to translate cultural values through the representation of what is considered human. The authors address museums' accountability for the histories of mannequin production and display in the West, and their responsibility to critically rethink how mannequins may be deployed in a self-aware and decolonial future for museums.

In the first chapter, "The Museum Mannequin as 'Body Without Organs'," art historian Jessica Stephenson provides a theoretical framework for mannequins through the lens of Deleuze and Guattari's philosophical concept introduced in the 1970s of the "body without organs," a virtual repository of potential that only becomes real once external forces impose themselves onto the potential. In this construct, Stephenson posits that this "body without organs" furthers our understanding of mannequins that are only activated once they've been dressed or contextualized through display. Focusing on "hyper-real life-cast mannequins," she further extends the body without organs ontology through her examination of "bushmen" mannequins originally created between 1907 and 1924, and then redisplayed in 2013 at the Iziko Sough African Museum in Cape Town, South Africa. Her chapter considers how the research, production, and display of these life-casts provide the vehicle to strip away the figures' personhood, while also bringing to bear the work of artist Pippa Skotnes and her installation, *Miscast: Negotiating the Presence of the Bushmen* from the late 1990s.

In the chapter that follows, "From Life?: Histories and Contemporary Perspectives on Modeling Native American Humankind Through Mannequins at the Smithsonian," anthropologist Gwyneira Isaac examines origins of mannequin life groups in the Bureau of Ethnology at the Smithsonian and also considers the contemporary contexts that they inhabit. These mannequins help viewers consider the extent to which complex intersections among art, science, and anthropology enable rethinking the divisions between scientific subscription to the Cartesian separation of mind and body, and artistic traditions, which are viewed as grounded in experiential knowledge. Rather than seeing these displays only through historic lenses, Isaac uses contemporary oral accounts to tell the stories of individuals who have been memorialized via mannequins in the name of science. Isaac addresses the creation process behind museum mannequins and the desires of their makers to achieve a high degree of "authenticity" – an insight that has remained hidden from the public.

Minou Schraven considers the impact of applying contemporary forensic techniques on ancient bodily remains in "Likeness and Likeability: Human Remains, Facial Reconstructions, and Identity-Making in Museum Displays." The power of this technology to "make the past come to life" is evident when museums and heritage sites include lifelike reconstructions of human remains in their displays. Schraven addresses the ethical implication of bodily reconstructions and the responses they elicit from visitors. Taking the reconstructions of Lindow Man at the British Museum and Yde Girl at the Drents Museum as examples, Schraven interrogates the meaning produced by comparing forensic reconstruction to tropes of lifelikeness and indexicality. She argues that the interpretations of their identities are dependent on the needs of the national and local desires of the communities that identify with them.

Using her curatorial work as an initial case study, Emma McClendon explores the use of mannequins in fashion exhibitions in the chapter "Fashion and Physique: Size, Shape, and Body Politics in the Display of Historical Dress." In discussing the planning process for her 2017 exhibition *The Body: Fashion and Physique*, McClendon highlights episodes from the history of fashion exhibitions to explore how certain types of mannequins and display practices became standardized. She argues that mannequin choices validate certain body types while perpetuating the marginalization of others. In this way, fashion exhibitions contribute to the construction of body image ideals by suggesting what types of bodies deserve to be visible and remembered.

Fashion historian Kyunghee Pyun examines the representation of Asian bodies through the display of mannequins in American museums in her chapter, "Asian Physiques of Mannequins in American Art Museums." Through interviews with exhibition designers, conservators, and curators at both art and natural history museums, the author creates a baseline from which to understand the representation of people of Asian descent through mannequins in museums and the logistical challenges that museum professionals face in creating these displays.

In "Figures of Speech: Black History at the National Great Blacks in Wax Museum," Bridget R. Cooks analyzes how the use of figurative forms in Baltimore, Maryland's most popular museum recognize the unbroken continuity of anti-Black violence and Black suffering while including moments of achievement. From a narrative walk through the great hall of national historical figures, the hull of an imagined slave ship, to the homages of twenty-first century icons, a visit to the museum is an intense emotional and educational experience. Cooks examines the function of the earnest museum that presents an Afrocentric Black history that is revelatory for most visitors.

In her chapter "Black is the Color of my True Love's Skin: The Symbolism and Significance of the Black Female Mannequin Figure in Mary Sibande's Creative Work," Lanisa Kitchiner explores how South African artist, Mary Sibande uses mannequins as a means to communicate alternative Black female narratives in select works from her exhibition, *Long Live the Dead Queen* (2010). Kitchiner asserts that Sibande intentionally constructs mannequin figures to celebrate and restore Black African female existence. She argues that Sibande's mannequins disrupt the archive of apartheid imagery to reject Eurocentric perceptions of beauty and the ideal human body. Sibande's mannequins work as powerful communicative tools that afford deeper understanding of and appreciation for how Black women imagine and reconstruct themselves in our hyper-racialized and grossly unjust world.

Collectively, the chapters of this book relay the complicated issues at stake when museums attempt to present race and cultural differences to their audiences. As the assertions of the #BlackLivesMatter, #DecolonizeThisMuseum, and #MuseumsAreNotNeutral movements challenge and generally perplex mainstream museum leadership, some directors and curators are facing the legacy of White supremacy and social hegemony.[15] In the last several years, American museum directors have disrupted regular acquisition and exhibition procedures in order to claim that Black Lives Matter in their institutions. Their efforts have been lauded and criticized. In April 2018, Christopher Bedford, director of the Baltimore Museum of Art (BMA), announced that the museum would deaccession seven art works, all by White men in their collection, in order to fund the accession of art by White women and artists of color. As a result, Bedford stated, "The BMA has now acquired 11 major works of art by women and artists of color purchased in full or in part with funds from the objects that were deaccessioned last spring. This is just one aspect of the museum's strategy to broaden the historical narrative of art and build a more diverse and inclusive art experience for Baltimore."[16] In February 2019, the San Francisco Museum of Modern Art followed the BMA's lead with the sale of a Mark Rothko painting to purchase works by artists of different racial and gender identities.[17] These are bold gestures by these museums, but they are also unsustainable. Transformational change to a museum's permanent collection can only occur with the funded support of museum boards and donors.

Notoriously conservative, the values of those in these powerful positions are often in conflict with the people who insist on equality, fair representation, and access to resources.[18]

In another instance in 2017, New York City mayor Bill de Blasio formed a committee to consider what should be done about several statues in the city that promote White supremacy. One of these is the troubling sculpture, *Equestrian Statue of Theodore Roosevelt* (1940) by James Earle Fraser, which has stood in front of the American Museum of Natural History since 1940. The statue shows a Native American man and a man of African descent who walk on either side of the president who rides on horseback. In 2019 the museum opened an exhibition called *Addressing the Statue* to educate visitors and invite them to share their thoughts about the promotion of the demeaning representation of Native American and Black people through Fraser's work. A month after public protest against police violence and anti-Black racism was sparked by the video recording of Minneapolis police officers murdering African American man, George Floyd, in May 2020, De Blasio ordered the removal of the statue. As of the beginning of 2021, the statue remains in place.

In 2020, directors of all four venues of the exhibition *Philip Guston Now* agreed to postpone the project over concerns that they had not communicated appropriately with Black constituents in preparation for the exhibit. In particular, the museum directors worried over the potential response by Black viewers to Guston's paintings that feature cartoonish Ku Klux Klan figures. The exhibition was planned to debut at the National Gallery of Art, Washington, DC in June 2020 before traveling to the Museum of Fine Arts, Houston, the Tate Modern in London, and the Museum of Fine Arts, Boston.[19] It is unclear how the museum directors expect the anti-Black climate in museums to change or why they believe it will improve by 2024. Suffice it to say, these museum leaders have agreed to pause their actions for a time of reflection and reconsideration.

We offer *Mannequins and Museums* as a resource in this moment of assessment of cultural institutions and museum values. We hope that it will provide clearer insight into the contexts in which mannequins were created and displayed and illuminate the tangible effects on the cultures they represent. Through the study of these life-size figures presented in the public sphere, we have the opportunity to better understand institutional desires to shape the stories of humankind.

## Notes

1 Tony Bennett, "The Exhibitionary Complex," *New Formations*, no. 4 (1988).
2 Bennett, "The Exhibitionary Complex," 73.

3 For a discussion of the formation of Native American mannequins and their life-groups at the National Museum of Natural History, see Gwyneira Isaac's chapter, "From Life?: Histories of and Contemporary Perspectives on Modeling Native American Humankind through Mannequins at the Smithsonian" in this volume.

4 For further reading on the history of Māori manikins in American museum displays see chapters three and four of Jennifer Wagelie, "Māori Art in America: The Display and Collection of Māori Art in the United States, 1802–2006," PhD Dissertation, Graduate Center, City University of New York, 2007.

5 Max Metz, "An Unanticipated Session at AAM 2017," June 11, 2017. https://sites.tufts.edu/museumstudents/2017/06/11/an-unanticipated-session-at-aam-2017/

6 See comments by The Descendant @Their_Child, May 8, 2017; Saleen Hue Penny @huedotart, May 9, 2017, and Dr. Lisa Gilbert @gilbertlisak, May 10, 2017.

7 See Tweet by Sam @museumsamSTL, May 10, 2017.

8 Abe, "Disabled Mannequins Was a Great Step," *RollingWithoutLimits.com*, July 23, 2014. www.rollingwithoutlimits.com/view-post/Disable-Mannequins-Was-a-Great-Step

9 Vivian Hendriksz, "Karen Millen Accused of Promoting 'Dangerous' Body Ideals with Too-Thin Mannequin," *FashionUnited.com*, March 12, 2015. https://fashionunited.uk/news/fashion/karen-millen-accused-of-promoting-dangerous-body-ideals-with-too-thin-mannequin/2015031215848

10 Marla Jo Fisher, "Say Goodbye to the Pirates of the Caribbean . . .," *OCRegister.com*, March 13, 2018. www.ocregister.com/2018/03/13/say-goodbye-to-the-pirates-of-the-caribbean-bride-auction-at-disneyland/

11 These two examples are particularly interesting for different reasons. Most of the people in the challenge with James and Obama are African American, making the moment of a posh celebration a counter to ethnographic dioramas that account for most museum representations of people of African descent. The McCarthy challenge is uncanny because there are already lifelike wax replicas of the iconic performer, making the actual live presence of McCarthy in the video harder to believe. See, "LeBron James and Cleveland Cavaliers Mannequin Challenge with First Lady Michelle Obama!," November 10, 2016. www.youtube.com/watch?v=5ZzklOEGW0w&feature=emb_logo; and "Paul McCartney #MannequinChallenge," November 16, 2016. www.youtube.com/watch?v=2INrQHCYuog

12 Emily Marshall Orr, Jake Yuzna, Margaret Russell, and Barbara Paris Gifford, *Ralph Pucci: Art of the Mannequin* (New York: Museum of Arts and Design, 2015).

13 Rosalind Williams, *Dream Worlds: Mass Consumption in Late Nineteenth-Century France* (Berkeley and Los Angeles: University of California Press, 1982); and Steven Heller and Louise Fili, *Counter Culture: The Allure of Mini-Mannequins* (Princeton: Princeton Architectural Press, 2001).

14 Jane Munro, *Silent Partners: Artist and Mannequin from Function to Fetish* (New Haven: Yale University Press, 2014); James W. Rauth, *Mannequin* (Terrace Park, OH: Wanoka Press, 2009); Richard P. Townsend, *Yinka Shonibare CBE at the Driehaus* (Chicago: Driehaus Museum, 2019); and Fred Wilson and Doro Globus, *Fred Wilson: A Critical Reader* (London: Ridinghouse Publishers, 2011).

15 See, Caroline Miranda, "Are Art Museums Still Racist?: The COVID Reset: *Los Angeles Times* Online, Last Modified, October 22, 2020, https://www.latimes.com/entertainment-arts/story/2020-10-22/art-museums-racism-covid-reset; LaTanya Autry and Mike Murawski, *Museums Are Not Neutral*, Last Modified, May 24, 2021, https://www.museumsarenotneutral.com/; Molly Enking, "'Decolonize This Place' Protesters Disrupt Brooklyn Museum, Condemn 'Imperial Plunder;" Gothamist, Last modified, April 30, 2018, https://gothamist.com/news/decolonize-this-place-protesters-disrupt-brooklyn-museum-condemn-imperial-plunder.

16 Nate Freeman, "A Controversial Deaccessioning has allowed the Baltimore Museum of Art to Buy New Works." *Artsy.net*, Last modified, December 20, 2018, https://www.artsy.net/news/artsy-editorial-controversial-deaccessioning-allowed-baltimore-museum-art-buy-new-works.

17 Sam Whiting, "SF MoMA Rothko Painting Sells for $50.1 Million," *Datebook*, May 17, 2019. https://datebook.sfchronicle.com/art-exhibits/sfmoma-rothko-painting-sells-for-50-1-million

18 An example of the conflict in values came to head when Warren B. Kanders, a vice chairperson of the Whitney Museum of American Art board was called out by protestors for his ownership of Safariland, a company that produces weapons and military supplies for law enforcement. Its materials are used at the United States-Mexico border and in domestic protests. See, Neda Ulaby, "At Whitney Museum Biennial, 8 Artists Withdraw in Protest of Link to Tear Gas Sales," *NPR.org*, July 21, 2019. www.npr.org/2019/07/21/743993348/at-whitney-museum-biennial-8-artists-withdraw-in-protest-of-link-to-tear-gas-sal; and Robin Pogrebin and Elizabeth A. Harris, "Warren Kanders Quits Whitney Board after Tear Gas Protests," *New York Times*, July 25, 2019. See also, Sarah Cascone, "Two Baltimore Museum Trustees Resign and Donors Rescind $50 Million in Gifts as the Institution Prepares to Sell Off Blue-Chip Art," *ArtnetNews.com*, October 26, 2020. https://news.artnet.com/art-world/baltimore-donors-rescind-50-million-gifts-1918139

19 Kaywin Feldman, Director, National Gallery of Art; Frances Morris, Director, Tate Modern; Matthew Teitelbaum, Ann and Graham Gund Director, Museum of Fine Arts Boston; and Gary Tenterow, Director, The Margaret Alkek Williams Chair, The Museum of Fine Arts, Houston, "*Phillip Guston Now:* Statement from the Directors," September 21, 2020. www.nga.gov/press/exh/5235.html; and Gareth Harris, "Directors of Tate, and the National Gallery of Art Defend Controversial Decision to Delay Philip Guston Show," *The Art Newspaper.com*, October 4, 2020.

# 1 The museum mannequin as "body without organs"

*Jessica Stephenson*

The museum mannequin reminds one of French philosophers Gilles Deleuze and Felix Guattari's concept of the "body without organs," that is, a virtual reservoir of potential (which could be a literal body, real or imagined, or more generally as the form that precedes content) that comes into being as external forces and flows act across this potential, activating certain possibilities and foreclosing others (1972). The "body without organs," in its highly variegated, yet distinct and intentional forms, demonstrates the absence of content until it takes in and reproduces the particular cultural milieus within which it is chosen to be embedded.

Equating the mannequin with the concept of "body without organs" elucidates the genres' ontology. Museum mannequins serve as supports for dress and other bodily adornments, or as descriptive prompts to flesh out broader display contexts, as for example when placed within diorama settings. They have no "organs," no content, no identity, until dressed or located within a contextual display. However, the hyper-realistic life-cast mannequin, a museum genre that rose to prominence in the nineteenth century and has endured into the twenty-first century, despite considerable criticism within public and museological circles, would appear to complicate the support function of the mannequin due to its appearance as simulated human body derived from once living individuals. Yet, as evident in this chapter, even the hyper-real life-cast mannequin only takes on identities or "content" as external forces act upon it. The reasons why this may be so are evidenced if we consider anthropologist Marzia Varutti's observation that the human body serves as the interface between the personal – the body as receptacle of individual subjectivity – and the social – the body as a signifier of one's place in society (2017). The human body can be understood both as the site of the self, as well as a catalyst for social relationships because, says Varutti, "it is evocative, symbolic and metaphoric, it can stand for other concepts, such as culture, race or gender. As a result, the body is a prime site of construction, contestation and negotiation of individual and collective

DOI: 10.4324/9780429260575-1

identities" (2017, 6). Varutti's observations apply not only to the human body, but also to its simulacra, as for example the museum mannequin. Petra Kuppers notes that "envisioning" bodies results in processes of "translation, interpretation, intervention" (2004, 125). Museum representations of bodies are thus constitutive and revelatory; envisioned bodies support specific viewpoints and express social imaginaries about those bodies' identities (Varutti, 2017).

This chapter offers an appraisal of the hyper-real life-cast museum mannequin as material process and as "body without organs" through discussion of a specific set of mannequins, created between 1907 and 1924, and then reproduced, repaired, and redisplayed until 2013 when they were deinstalled from exhibit within the South African Museum, today known as the Iziko South African Museum, Cape Town, South Africa. I argue that the life-cast mannequin provides a surface upon which numerous social constructs may be imprinted. I consider how it is that the research into, production of, and multiple display moments of these life-casts afforded a means by which to strip away the models' personhood; impressions of their bodies were transferred to paint and plaster as they took on various "imaginaries" within the museum.

Over the course of a century of manufacture and display, these particular mannequins have passed through five distinct museological phases, with additional ones yet to come. Museum mannequins may have many "senses of self," those traced here include their identity as "specimens" and "fetishes," instruments of racial and scientific physical inquiry and sexual fantasy; as "artifacts," props for ethnological theory, theatre, and political propaganda; as "historical documents," witnesses to historical moments, practices, and persons; "art objects," sites for activism and museum critique; and as "surrogate persons," claimed ancestors and physical evidence for genocide and human suffering. To trace the history of life-cast mannequins over the course of the twentieth and twenty-first centuries is thus also to trace shifts in museum ethos; dialogic study reveals that specific museological practices and display techniques – here the simulated body as pliable object in the service of constructed representations of race, gender, culture, and class – endure, shift, change, and are contested. The layers of meaning that accrue to their surfaces eventually led to a reclaiming of personhood, in the sense that the mannequins have recently become surrogates for lost bodies, peoples, and personal and collective histories.

Photographic reproductions of the mannequins in question are intentionally excluded from this chapter, written at a moment when they remain off display, their futures up for debate as objects signifying complex genealogical and epistemological connections between the past and the present, the dead and the living, ancestors and descendants (Schramm, 2016, 131).

Currently, museum officials and representatives of certain Khoisan groups regard the mannequins to be human remains, not of "specimens" but of "ancestors."[1] They are also, as Schramm observes, "material evidence to . . . (the) destruction, dispossession, and scientific objectification" of individuals (2016, 138). In what follows, the history of mannequin production and display at the South African Museum is described, but is intentionally withheld from visual consumption in deference to prior and current criticisms by certain scholars and Khoisan that to do so repeats a violence otherwise described in this text (Douglas and Law, 1997; Bregin, 2001).

The life-casts were made under the auspices of Louis Péringuey, then director of the museum, and his team, most notably, taxidermist and museum modeler James Drury, in a quest to capture and fix a physical impression of what Péringuey, writing in the early twentieth century, termed "pure-bred" or "pure-blood Bush People," those labeled within colonial culture as Bushman or Hottentot, designations applied to groups of people then perceived to share certain unique linguistic, physical, and lifestyle traits and today known through self-designations as Khoisan (Davison, 1993; Skotnes, 2002).[2] Between 1907 and 1924 Drury photographed, measured and made field-molds of eighty-eight so-called "pure-bred" Khoisan living in far-flung regions from Prieska, Carnarvon, and other villages of the Northern Cape to Grootfontein and Sandfontein in southwest Africa (Namibia), Kanye in the Bechuanaland Protectorate (Botswana), and Lake Chrissie area in eastern Transvaal. Fourteen of the individuals whose bodies were recorded were incarcerated at the time. Back at the museum, the field-molds of sixty eight people were cast in plaster and carefully painted to convey a sense of realism and exactitude (Davison, 1993), the purpose underpinning the project being to capture the imprint of a perceived dying race, as is evident in an excerpt from one of Péringuey's letters, in which he requested the blessing of the Cape Government:

> Sir,
>
> Owing to the rapid disappearance by reasons which I need not mention here, of the pure specimens of Hottentot and Bushmen races the Trustees of the Museum are endevouring to obtain models from the living flesh which would enable the exact physical reproduction of the survivors of these nearly extinguished races.
>
> (in Davison, 1993, 168)

Here, the life-cast mannequin functions as effigy, which, as Sandberg notes, served as one "tangible manifestation of a wider array of circulating corporeal traces and effects" designed to stand in for actual persons and at the same time offering "new possibilities for imagining space and time" (2003, 5). Wax figures, notes Weber, and ethnographic objects including life-cast mannequins, are such replacements. Along with photography and film, the life-cast mannequin implicitly conveys that those depicted are temporally and spatially absent (2016, 305).

Péringuey sent Drury to Kanye in 1908 to collect data, make life-molds, and collect Indigenous material culture. He armed Drury with very specific criteria:

> For Drury – memorandum about the modelling
>
> I would like to have first, a group of five or six men, women and children photographed in the position they naturally assume, either sitting down, or as if they were on the march: the men carrying his few arms and chattels; the women carrying what they generally carry, the youngsters carry nothing . . . make them assume positions that will not make the models appear too stiff . . . try to place them in such a position that would not prove too fatiguing, in order avoid also stiffness in the reproductions. . . . Pay special attention to the hairs in your note of the specimens, of the colour or expression of the eye, of the shape of the ear, and above all copy the colour of the skin, and verify your slab a couple of days after you have painted it in order to make quite sure of the genuine colour. . . . Men are of course desirable, women more so. You will be careful to take all their peculiarities, including the "apron." A special moulding of the same to be added to the statue is very much wanted.
>
> (in Davison, 1993, 172)

Capturing the imprint of live "specimens" with all the "racial" data of skin tone, texture, hair, and other features in the form of the life-cast mannequins formed part of a larger project to document a "dying race" to include the collection, generally under ethically dubious circumstances, of human remains from graves which Péringuey referred to as "relics" (Legassick and Rassool, 1999, 31).[3] The South African Museum project thus conforms to a much longer history – the popular and scientific fixation on the Bushman body (Gordon, 1992), which can be traced back to at least the early 1800s through the tragic example Sara Baartman. Taken from her native homeland in the Cape Colony in 1810, Baartman was paraded and prodded on stages in London and France as the Hottentot Venus, a living curiosity, exemplar of the Bushman race defined by her steatopygic buttocks and female "apron" – elongated labia. She was subjected to close physical scrutiny in life and after death, when her brain, skeleton, and genitals were retained for further study and her body "preserved" through a cast made after her death. It was shown at a French museum until 1974 alongside her reconstructed skeleton. The vitrine tombstone identified the mannequin and skeleton as "La Vénus

Hottentote," belying the conceptual shift performed within the museum where reconstructed skeletal remains and mannequin as simulacra represent imposed constructs – they are specimens of gender, race, and sexual perversion, they are not Sara Baartman herself.

In both Sara Baartman's case and those who "participated" in the South African Museum project, the transfer of living flesh to molded wax and cast plaster entailed a reduction of an individual, a person, to a physical racial type through a stripping away of social context and personal biography. Names, living conditions, and contemporary material culture were not recorded by Drury in the field. Further, the mannequins' museum accession records support their typological purpose, only recording a description of the mannequin's appearance, the model's sex, area of origin, and racial designation according to colonial academic classifications. The modeler and casters name (Drury) are also given, thereby drawing attention to the mannequin as crafted object (Davison, 1993, 174).[4]

Within the museum context, the life-cast fulfills the function of relic (in a quite literal sense for Baartman who had passed before a mold was made of her body). Per Pérignuey's instructions, they were designed to defy artifice (stiffness), to appear life-like; they nevertheless serve as literal death masks, not of specific individuals, but of the "purebred Bushman," a perceived fast disappearing physical type that, in the context of the museum's mission to document and preserve, could be "saved" from loss through life-like simulacra. The choice of life-cast to fulfill this goal was critical: although mannequins are inanimate things, they often appear eerily alive to the viewer (Weber, 2016, 303). The poses assumed by each are unique and striking, designed to persuade, the delicate coloring of the skin intended to be realistic, details such as hair, wrinkles, veins, and nails contributing clinical precision, implying objectivity, but of course Péringuey's letters and memos reveal the staged nature of the entire enterprise.

The negation of personal and cultural information in favor of physical context and classification as "specimen" was further enacted through the mannequins' display location within the vicinity of the museum's faunal collection. A selection, grouped in a tableau with minimal scenery hinting at a vague geographical location and titled *Karoo Diorama*, went on public display in 1915 (Davison, 1998, 144). Even though placed in a group, the figures did not interact with each other or with their surroundings. Some figures were positioned towards and others posed facing away from the viewer (Legassick and Rassool, 1999, 5). The viewer's focus on naked body parts was amplified by the scantily clad figures wearing nothing but diminutive loincloths and through their position at a raised elevation bringing the midsection of the body to the viewers eye level. The exhibit label invited close viewing of the mannequins as exemplars of a now absent race:

> CAPE BUSHMEN: The Bushmen of the Cape appear to have been the purest-blooded representatives of the Bushman stock, much purer than those of the Kalahari and other more northerly districts. They are now practically extinct. They were light in colour and of small or medium height; the prominent posterior development (steatopygy) of the women was a characteristic feature of the race.
>
> To anthropologists the Bushmen are one of the most interesting races in the world. There are strong grounds for suspecting that they are of the same stock as the remote Upper Palaeolithic period. This cannot yet be definitely asserted but recent discoveries in North and East Africa have tended to strengthen the probability considerably.
>
> (in Davison, 2001, 15)

The life-casts moved between various displays into the 1950s, with amendments made through the addition of dress. These additions were noted on the life-casts' accession cards, reflecting the shifting status of the mannequins as both physical specimens, but also now as "artifacts" – cultural prototypes – through their location within the newly named *Bushman Room* and *New Ethnology Gallery*. Although the figures were generally more fully clothed, they continued to stand out singly within grouped displays, with labels placed at the foot of each figure to identify it by race, sex, and place of origin.

In 1959, under the guidance of museum ethnologist Margaret Shaw, fourteen mannequins were brought together within a descriptive habitat diorama to depict life within a hunter-gatherer settlement. This diorama context fully ushered in a second "sense of self" for the life-casts as ethnological "artifacts," examples of a specific cultural archetype – namely the "hunter-gatherer" conceived as child of nature, modern humankind's living Stone Age ancestor. The mannequins' newly acquired identity reflects the interests of an emerging salvage anthropology alongside the official entrenchment of apartheid in South Africa, with its political agenda of racial and cultural difference that underpinned the policy of separate development.

The *Bushman Diorama* was situated between the *Hall of Man* and the *Ethnology Gallery* which linked the life-casts with surrounding displays of African material culture and artifacts associated with "ancient man." The diorama's scene was loosely based on an aquatint titled *Bosjemans Frying Locusts* by Samuel Daniel and published in the book *African Scenery and Animals* (1804–1805), as well as on descriptions of /Xam hunter-gatherer lifeways detailed in the journals of J. Barrow and W. Somerville, nineteenth century travelers to the Karoo (Summers, 1975). These representations gained currency in the mid-twentieth century in response to changing academic and popular perceptions of Bushmen, by then renamed, at least in academic circles, as San or Khoisan. In a post-World War II world, the interest in human ecology recast the Bushmen as children of nature, the Stone Age living ancestor of modern humankind. This image found favor within anthropological and popular culture spheres out of nostalgia for the values associated with the hunter-gatherer culture as symbol of egalitarian pre-modern humanity (van der Post, 1958; Wilmsen, 1989; Barnard, 1989).

The mannequins collectively formed part of a cohesive scene depicting a camp of hunter-gatherers going about their daily activities while a flock of birds flew overhead. A theatrical moment is captured, the figure of a young boy points towards the birds, an adult male figure stands ready with bow and arrow to take a shot while another readies himself to do the same. Women either watch the men or go about their daily activities; one female figure rests within a reed shelter. All wear only diminutive front aprons to show off the figures' physical features, particularly steatopygia.

The illusionistic representational techniques and real elements (body casts, clothing, jewelry, and utilitarian implements) contained within the diorama tricked the eye into believing that the scene was real, existing in the time and space occupied by the viewer. The painted background and floor covered with gravel, rocks, and plant matter enhanced the appearance of an actual landscape, while overhead lighting simulated sunlight. Yet, containing the figures behind glass reminded the viewer that the scene is non-threatening and removed from their own space and time, while drawing them in to enjoy closer inspection. Positioning the mannequins at an oblique angle to the glass, and thus to the viewer, also made for a non-threatening experience, as the life-casts look off and out without making eye contact. Encountering the mannequins within the diorama thus becomes a game, a safe estrangement, the viewer is afforded an intimate view of an idealized exotic African community living in an undefined place and time. The diorama offers a scene set in space, but frozen in time, ahistorical. Through this spatial and temporary estrangement and negation of historical facts, the diorama and attendant life-casts supported the political and ideological imaginary of apartheid – as did the label installed when the exhibit opened in 1960:

> A CAPE BUSHMAN CAMP IN THE KAROO: This diorama shows some activities of hunter-gatherers. The viewer should imagine that a flock of birds has flown overhead and attracted the attention of the group. With the exception of a few in Gordonia, there are no Bushmen living in the Cape. The figures shown here are PLASTER CASTS of living people aged between 18 and 60 excepting the man making fire who was alleged to have been about 100. They were nearly all living

> in Prieska and Carnarvon districts. The casts were made by Mr James Drury, modeler at the museum from 1902 to 1942.
>
> (in Davison, 2001, 17)

The reader is left to assume that this scene represents the only way Bushmen people would have lived, and furthermore that their lifeways were all but extinct, preserved only through these simulated bodies – "artifacts" of a lost past. While obfuscating the living conditions of those cast in favor of a romantic notion of Bushmen as hunter-gatherers, the text nevertheless lends credibility to its "historical" accuracy by recording the purported ages of the individuals cast. Although the diorama was meant to render cultural information in the most accessible realistic three-dimensional manner, it, along with the mannequins within, elicit imaginative engagements that override the pragmatic and scientific facts that the display was called upon to convey. As Weber notes,

> Such exhibits may inadvertently evoke spontaneous fantasizing although they are designed to render facts. As facts and fictions intermingle in them, mannequins have the potential to puzzle us with their tangible and life-sized human form and to confront us with an ontological and hermeneutic conundrum.
>
> (2016, 303)

By one and the same gesture, the diorama and mannequin serve as records of geographic and cultural information as well as evidence of physical absence. Cultural historian Britta Lange therefore identifies such objects as examples of the contradictions inherent within ethnology (and I might add, the museum), specifically the intent to depict absent cultures while appealing to the idea of their presence within the museum space (Weber, 2016, 305).

As the diorama's opening coincided with the official entrenchment of apartheid in South Africa, the life-casts within took on political overtones as "artifacts" in support of cultural and racial difference, the criteria on which the bedrock of separate development based itself. Further inscribing this ideology is the fact that, in the 1960s, the colonial-era European collection was transferred from the South African Museum to the nearby Cultural History Museum, while the Bushman Diorama remained behind alongside exhibits of stuffed animals and birds. At the time, African material culture fell within the purview of physical anthropology and racial studies, part of "natural history." Physical examples of African cultures, classified as "ethnology," were thus conceptually separated from cultural history, identified as white colonial history, a divide that supported apartheid political policy.[5]

From the mid-1970s onwards, the association of the life-casts with natural history became a key issue of criticism within museum circles (Davison, 2018). The political context of apartheid South Africa added cogency to the criticism that the location of the diorama and mannequins within the context of natural history rather than cultural history was racist in conception. As a result, the diorama underwent a number of changes to reflect shifting paradigms with an increased emphasis on situating the life-casts within historical contexts. In 1988, a new exhibit label read:

> In the early nineteenth century /Xam hunter-gatherers lived in the semi-arid Karoo. From hill-top camps they could watch the movement of game on the plains and spot the approach of enemies. Their way of life was shaped by the seasonal availability of edible plants, water and movements of game. To avoid overusing food and water supplies /Xam bands ranged widely within hunting territories which were defined by recognized landmarks. By the mid-nineteenth century most hunter-gatherers in the Karoo had been killed in fighting with advancing colonists and displaced khoikhoi. The survivors were drawn into colonial society as labourers and servants.
>
> (in Davison, 1991, 163)

In addition, in 1989 curators installed an exhibit beside the *Bushman Diorama* to address the history of the mannequin as institutional vehicle in the service of objectifying individuals, cultures, races, and genders. Didactic in intent, the exhibit presented a biography of the mannequins on display – who made them, when, how, and why, thus anchoring the objects to a history of museum practice. The display also connected the life-casts to the individuals from whose bodies they were made. The mannequins' "sense of self" was thus reframed as "historical document" through a series of five panels that collectively formed an exhibit titled *About the Diorama.* The panels described the history of the diorama, explaining how it served as a major attraction, and juxtaposing the dire colonial history of the individuals who modelled for the casts against the commodification and romanization of Bushmen as archetypes performed by fiction writers and anthropologists.[6]

The exhibit also included a single mannequin, identified as a representation of Lys Achterdam. A reproduction of Lys's body was also on display, near-naked, in the adjacent *Bushman Diorama*, as it had been for over seventy years, while the duplicate mannequin within the *About the Diorama* exhibit showed her wearing colonial period dress and thus as she appears in photographs taken in 1911, the year her body was originally cast. Including a mannequin dressed in period clothing, identified by name and to document a personal history effectively broke the anonymous and ahistorical narrative afforded by the diorama, ushering in a third identity for the mannequin as "historical document." As Weber argues, the lack of personal information constitutes a major point of critique for the mannequin because such a depersonalized mode of representation is not only guided by, but also invites an objectifying perspective in viewer contemplation (2016, 306). The appearance of a clothed and named Lys Achterdam complicates this mannequin's purpose due to the cast persons' absence owing to death. As the individuals who serve as models may have been alive at the moment when their likeness was taken, their personal historicity associates them with death, and as a result the ontological condition of life-cast mannequins inevitably shifts, over time, to become memorabilia of the deceased (Weber, 2016). The duplicate mannequin of Lys Agterdam thus shifts the mannequin from transmitting racial scientific information to conveying personal information as a *memento mori*.

Yet, as Cape Town-based artist Pippa Skotnes observed of museum docents, tour guides, schoolteachers, parents, and children visiting the *Bushman Diorama* during the early 1990s, the *About the Diorama* history display went largely unnoticed; visitors favored the timeless trope offered by the *Bushman Diorama* (Skotnes, 2015, 49).

Skotnes curated an exhibition/art installation in 1996 at the nearby South African National Gallery called *Miscast: Negotiating the Presence of the Bushmen* to confront the South African Museum's *Bushman Diorama* with the objects, visual materials, and documents housed in museum storerooms, libraries, and archives to tell a very different story of Khoisan engagement with colonialism and modernity. The exhibit presented the viewer with visual and textual media by which to bridge the conceptual gap between mannequin, diorama, and the actual historical processes of conflict and marginalization experienced by those cast. This intention was achieved by collapsing the space between museum storeroom, archive, and exhibition, drawing attention to the tension between what is exhibited, deemed acceptable for public consumption, and what remains hidden, stored in museum storerooms, not fit for public display. In so doing the artist invites the viewer to look into the Bushman mannequins – visually, conceptually, and historically – as art objects. *Miscast* also presented a mix of reproduced texts and images in order to destabilize the teleological historical narrative of the documentary display, *About the Diorama*, by juxtaposing and mixing a diverse range of material that, according to the curator/artist "structured into the form of the exhibit a high degree of multivalency so it would be more about knowledge in the making than a presentation of the already known" (Skotnes, 2001, 313). Indeed, the purposeful lack of chronology in the exhibition, according to Skotnes, intended to problematize the processes of selecting information and gathering it into a seamless narrative as occurs in the diorama. "I tried to suggest that history is always fragmentary and incomplete and that histories are, like displays, always temporary and contingent, endlessly able to be reshaped by new insights" (Skotnes, 2001, 314).

Situated at the center of the gallery, a stack of rifles, chained together and mounted on a cross-shaped structure, evoked what the artist described as "tomb, prison, church, and fort." Positioned at the corners of this structure, plaster death-casts of decapitated human heads, trophies taken in colonial wars and as punishment for cattle theft, presented a stark exposé of the lives and fate of peoples labeled Bushman. Nearby, thirteen platforms elevated piece-mold fragments of human torsos and limbs, the byproducts of Drury's original casting project. By situating fragments, elements from the mannequin production process, around the trophy heads and the "tomb, prison, church and fort," the historical factors motivating the need to document this "fast disappearing race of peoples" through mannequin production were alluded to. Their raw, brittle, broken, and ephemeral physical state, evidence of the wear and tear on the body in the process of creation, also drew attention to the artifice of the mannequins. Here the mannequin is not only an object of desire or ethnological inquiry and fantasy, but equally a physical site of suffering, pain, and death.

The fragmentation of the figure ushers in associations of human fragility, moving the viewer into the realm of art, feeling, and empathy. Configured in elegant arrangements and dramatically isolated by shadow and light, the fragments become sensual, almost classical in their aesthetics, intensified by the warm glow of gallery lights on their surfaces (Kasfir, 1997). The cool, clinical objectivity encountered in prior mannequin displays is replaced here by unease, as the viewer encounters a slippage from aesthetic beauty into abject horror with the nearby glass exhibition cabinet containing diagrams of body parts, bottled molds of physical specimens, and dissecting and measuring instruments, references to the brutal effects of scientific and racial typology projects. These effects were most overtly communicated by additional mannequin piece-mold parts found beyond, arranged in a haphazard pile, and starkly lit by florescent light, spread out like discarded physical dissections or horrific remnants of war, triggering visual images of genocides and holocaust. As one exhibition reviewer observed, here to see was "the . . . metaphorical remains of desiccated Khoisan bodies, filleted and defleshed to provide the 'meat' of Western science" (Lane, 1996, 7). Beyond the pile of dismembered limbs, banks of museum storage boxes with labels drew attention to things collected but never displayed. For example, one label read: "Human Remains: Not Suitable for Display." Another stated, "Koos Sas was killed for resisting arrest. His skull was sent to the Physiology Department, University of Stellenbosch, and postcard images of the dead Koos Sas are sold in aid of the Afrikaans Christian Women's Organization" (Lane, 1996, 6–7).

While the South African Museum molds were painted by Drury to simulate living flesh in the pursuit of science and illusion, the piece-mold fragments shown in the *Miscast* show were left in a raw, plastic state as illustrations of technical processes in the service of visual fictions. Live-cast mannequins are made through a process of deconstruction and reconstruction. It is impossible to live-cast a body whole, as a result Drury cast his subject's bodies in pieces, pulling as many as ten to sixteen piece-molds from each body, then meticulously assembling them into a whole (Rau, 1964). Skotnes reverses the process of mannequin production, destroying the unified mannequin in order to critique the very conditions and motivations guiding its production. Contrary to the affirmative and illusionistic mannequin resident within the *Bushman Diorama*, she offers a critical vision of the mannequin casting method as a process that fragments bodies, individuals, communities, and histories. Unlike the *Bushman Diorama* with its cohesive idyllic narrative and hyper-real mannequins, Skotnes' vision is dark and pessimistic, illustrating "how technological replicas of the body dismantle life in the service of portraying it accurately" (Weber, 2016, 307).

Juxtaposed against these bodily fragments, the site of pain, suffering, and loss, ran a parallel text, presented through archival photographs and material culture. Mirroring the thirteen platforms housing anonymous mannequin body parts, appeared thirteen cases containing objects of Khoisan manufacture – hats, walking sticks, divination discs, hunting equipment, and body adornments, the very same kinds of objects featured on the mannequins, but here enshrined in velvet-lined boxes, like sacred relics. Each case was dedicated to a known San person: Dikwain, //Kabbo, Sara Bartman, and other men and women whose traces can be excavated from historical records. Skotnes writes of this display as a "Last Supper in which named individuals were sacrificed in the interests of the pervasive display of a collective racial type" (Skotnes, 2002, 264).

*Miscast* foregrounded the troubling nexus between colonial violence, science, and museum representations of Khoisan people through its explicit focus on the objectified Indigenous body and its fragmentation into casts, bones, body parts, and abstract measurements (Skotnes, 1996). Despite its explicit artistic mission, numerous critics denounced the exhibition for repeating the violence against Indigenous bodies, putting them once again on display for visual consumption (Douglas and Law, 1997; Bregin, 2001; Jackson and Robins, 1999). San delegates found the display of naked, mutilated bodies deeply offensive. Mario Mahango, community leader of the !Xun San, observed that the display constituted another act of violence. "[People who] show these things here," he said, "[are] just as bad as the people who did those things long ago."[7]

In 2001, the *Bushman Diorama* was closed in response to the public outrage sparked by *Miscast* as well as an appeal made by Nelson Mandela that South African museums strive to launch exhibitions meaningful to all members of the new South Africa (Abraham, 2004; Wakeham, 2008). The exhibit remained curtained off within the museum gallery for over a decade until 2013 when it was deinstalled and moved into storage. The decision to remove the casts from public display occurred after a lengthy review by museum officials and Indigenous communities. As a result, the life-casts have taken on a fifth, current "sense of self" as "surrogate persons," claimed ancestors, and unethically acquired imprints of human bodies. As Schramm notes, casts, photographs, voice recordings, life-measurements, and human remains together form part and parcel of racial anthropology (2016). In the reasoning put forward by museum officials and Indigenous representatives for removing the mannequins from public view they are now considered to be intimate material embodiments of racial anthropology and violence, the products of coercion, objectification, and the desecration of graves (Schramm, 2016, 133). In June 2011 it was determined that all body casts made by James Drury should be deemed human remains because, through the very act of casting, traces of bodily material (hair, cells, DNA) had transferred to the molds and casts. They thus contain actual parts of a deceased person and are not mere representations (Rassool, 2015, 662–663).[8] The life-casts are now embedded in a network of meanings that confirm newly reclaimed Khoisan identities in a post-apartheid period, with repatriation and reburial on the table, once a process for identifying descendent claimants is put in place. As such, the life-cast mannequins made by Drury continue to exist as "body without organs," reservoirs of potential that acquire identities as external forces and flows act across their surfaces, demonstrating the absence of content until they take in and reproduce the specific contexts within which they are embedded.

The museum mannequin as a "body without organs" is a site of possibility that, time and again, is implanted with "organs," identities inscribed and recorded upon it. The identities traced here include specimen, fetish, artifact, historical document, art object, and human remains. By its very nature as a "body without organs," the museum mannequin is a site for the realization of something else, as the "organs" or identities imposed upon it become something new: the life-like image is a death mask, the artifact a fantasy, the historical document an illusion, and the material object more than simulacrum, containing as it does traces of human DNA. Life-cast mannequins, existing as they do in a perpetual state of becoming, call us to question what we have previously known.

## Notes

1 Khoisan is the term for Indigenous peoples of Southern Africa who self-identify as non-Bantu speaking Africans.
2 Peringuey received the blessing of the Cape Government to cast prisoners in several locations when he wrote in 1907:

> Sir,
> Owing to the rapid disappearance, by reasons which I need not mention here, of the pure specimens of Hottentot and Bushmen races the Trustees of the Museum are endevouring to obtain models from the living flesh which would enable the exact physical reproduction of the survivors of these nearly extinguished races.
>
> (in Davison, 2001, 11)

3 The ethically unstable terrain here is not surprising when one considers the following example, taken from a letter written by Péringuey to government official A. R. Wilmot on September 28, 1909. "[T]he relics should be simply dug out . . . and if well besprinkled with paraffin . . . and left to the action of the sun in the veld – of course in a box – for a few days, it would not prove offensive and could be sent by rail – contents of the package of course not divulged but termed specimen of natural history" (Legassick and Rassool, 1999, 41).
4 For example, museum accession number AP3398 identifies the mannequin as: (sex) Female, (group) !Kung, (description), Old woman standing, (locality) Nuragas (Davison, 1993, 176).
5 Patricia Davison conducted a survey of some seventy odd visitors to the museum to ascertain public perception of the diorama. She found that visitors associated the casts "with taxidermy" suggesting viewers believed that the figures were preserved and stuffed for display like the animals to be seen elsewhere in the museum. Half of the visitors thought the diorama depicted the early nineteenth century; 25% believed it was placed in "no specific time" and 16% believed it portrayed the early twentieth century. Nine percent dated its representation to the present (Davison, 1991, 207).
6 As observed by the author on a visit to the South African Museum in 1997.
7 Comments by Mario Mahango at the National Gallery, Cape Town, April 14, 1996.
8 The return in 2002 of Sara Baartman's skeletal remains along with the mannequin made from body molds is a powerful precedent, with the mannequin being buried along with her bones.

## References

Abrahams, Y. *Final Summary Report, Iziko Museums Consultation Process*, November 30, 2004. Mimeo.

Barnard, A. "The Lost Word of Laurens van der Post?" *Current Anthropology* 30, no. 1 (1989): 104–114.

Bregin, E. "Miscast: Bushmen in the Twentieth Century." *Current Writing* 13, no. 1 (2001): 87–107.

Davison, P. "Material Culture Context and Meaning: A Critical Investigation of Museum Practice." Unpublished thesis submitted for degree of Doctor of Philosophy in the Department of Archaeology, Cape Town: University of Cape Town, 1991.

Davison, P. "Human Subjects as Museum Objects: A Project to Make Life-Casts of 'Bushmen' and 'Hottentots', 1907–1924." *Annals of the South African Museum* 102, no. 5 (1993): 165–183.

Davison, P. "Museums and the Reshaping of Memory." In *Negotiating the Past: The Making of Memory in South Africa*, edited by S. Nuttall and C. Coetzee, 165–183. Cape Town: Oxford University Press, 1998.

Davison, P. "Typecast: Representations of the Bushmen at the South African Museum." *Public Archaeology* 2, no. 1 (2001): 3–20.

Davison, P. "The Politics and Poetics of the Bushman Diorama at the South African Museum." *ICOFOM Study Series* 46 (2018): 81–97.

Deleuze, G., and F. Guattari. *Anti-Oedipus: Çapitalism and Schizophrenia*. Translated by R. Hurley, M. Seem, and H.R. Lane. London and New York: Continuum, 1972.

Douglas, S., and L. Law. "Beating around the Bush(man!): Reflections on 'Miscast: Negotiating Khoisan History and Material Culture'." *Visual Anthropology* 10, no. 1 (1997): 85–108.

Gordon, R. "The Venal Hottentot Venus and the Great Chain of Being." *African Studies* 51, no. 2 (1992): 85–201.

Jackson, S., and S. Robins. "Miscast: The Place of the Museum in Negotiating the Bushman Past and Present." *Critical Arts* 13, no. 1 (1999): 69–101.

Kasfir, S. "Cast, Miscast: The Curator's Dilemma." *African Arts* 33, no. 1 (1997): 1, 4, 6, 8–9, 93.

Kuppers, P. "Visions of Anatomy: Exhibitions and Dense Bodies." *Differences: A Journal of Feminist Cultural Studies* 15, no. 3 (2004): 123–156.

Lane, P. "Breaking the Mould? Exhibiting Khoisan in Southern African Museums." *Anthropology Today* 12, no. 5 (1996): 45–55.

Legassick, M., and C. Rassool. *Skeletons in the Cupboard: Museums and the Incipient Trade in Human Remains, 1907–1917*. Bellville, Cape Town: University of the Western Cape, 1999.

Rassool, C. "Re-Storing the Skeletons of Empire: Return, Reburial and Rehumanisation in Southern Africa." *Journal of Southern African Studies* 41, no. 3 (2015): 653–670.

Rau, R. "How James Drury Cast the Bushman Displayed at the South African Museum." *South African Journal of Science* (1964): 242–244.

Sandberg, M. *Living Pictures, Missing Persons*. Princeton: Princeton University Press, 2003.

Schramm, K. "Casts, Bones and DNA: Interrogating the Relationship between Science and Postcolonial Indigeneity in Contemporary South Africa." *Anthropology Southern Africa* 39, no. 2 (2016): 131–144.

Skotnes, P. *Miscast: Negotiating the Presence of the Bushmen*. Cape Town: University of Cape Town Press, 1996.

Skotnes, P. "Civilized Off the Face of the Earth: Museum Display and the Silencing of the/Xam." *Poetics Today* 22, no. 2 (2001): 299–321.

Skotnes, P. "The Politics of Bushman Representations." In *Images and Empires: Visuality in Colonial and Post-Colonial Africa*, edited by P. Landau and D. Kaspin, 130–145. Berkeley: University of California Press, 2002.

Skotnes, P. "Fugitive Archive: A Response to the Bushman Diorama." In *Uncertain Curature: In and Out of the Archive*, edited by C. Hamilton and P. Skotnes, 47–61. Johannesburg, South Africa: Jacana, 2015.

Summers, R. *A History of the South African Museum 1825–1975*. Cape Town: Balkema, 1975.

van der Post, L. *The Lost World of the Kalahari*. New York: Harcourt Brace, 1958.

Varutti, M. "Materializing the Past: Mannequins, History and Memory in Museums: Insights from the Northern European and East-Asian Contexts." *Nordisk Museologi* 1 (2017): 5–20.

Wakeham, P. *Taxidermic Signs: Reconstructing Aboriginality*. Minneapolis: University of Minnesota Press, 2008.

Weber, D. "Vivifying the Uncanny: Ethnographic Mannequins and Exotic Performers in Nineteenth-Century German Exhibition Culture." In *Fact and Fiction: Literary and Scientific Cultures in Germany and Britain*, edited by C. Lehleiter, 298–331. Toronto: University of Toronto Press, 2016.

Wilmsen, E. *Land Filled with Flies*. Chicago: Chicago University Press, 1989.

# 2 From life?

## Histories and contemporary perspectives on modeling Native American humankind through mannequins at the Smithsonian

*Gwyneira Isaac*

### Shelf life: dissonance between past and present models of anthropology exhibits

In the not-so-distant past, the anthropology galleries of the National Museum of Natural History (NMNH) at the Smithsonian Institution were home to a series of dioramas using mannequins and life-groups to depict cultural diversity around the world. To some, these displays evoked fond memories of the museums of their childhood. To others the oddly static figures with dust-coated-hair were uncomfortable survivors of an archaic display style that needed more than just a physical cleaning – but an ideological reboot around how race and culture should be represented and by whom. Their origin stories as well as their contemporary uses prompt an examination of issues that stem from the tensions created during the making of these mannequins between curators and community members around scientific and institutional research agendas, and issues of personal and cultural identity. These interwoven and conflicting histories also evoke tensions between concepts of trust and coercion, makers and models, revealing who in fact is given power to physically materialize humankind and/or humanity in the museum display context.

Debates in the NMNH over the fate of these mannequins has divided opinions between those who see them as museum props that should be destroyed, versus those who view them as preservation-worthy specimens dating back to the beginning of museum anthropology in the nineteenth century. At the same time, plans to redo the anthropology halls stalled due to changing priorities at both the NMNH and the wider Smithsonian. By 2002, the historic anthropology life-groups and dioramas had been removed – not in order to rebuild or re-examine how to display anthropological knowledge in the twenty-first century – but to make way for the new Sant Ocean Hall, which now showcases NMNH research on marine diversity. Subsequently, the relocated mannequins remained in the museum basement until 2011,

DOI: 10.4324/9780429260575-2

when they were either disposed of due to their poor condition, or re-shelved in the anthropology department collections facility in Maryland. They now rest among the physical anthropology collections, awaiting either disposal or to be catalogued into the collections. As such, they occupy a liminal space between belonging and estrangement – existing as neither museum specimens nor ephemera. Their current status also reflects the larger landscape in which anthropology's presence in the NMNH galleries mirrors this liminality, due to how the discipline has moved into a critical examination of the study of race and the conversations around social justice issues, yet natural history museum display techniques have either fallen behind, or are entirely absent.

The only vestige of an anthropological footprint that remains in what became the Ocean Hall is the figure of an Inuit hunter hanging from the ceiling in a kayak, as if magically suspended between the museum's earthly and heavenly worlds (Figure 2.1). Unlike the previous anthropology mannequins of the 1880s, this one is based on a visiting Smithsonian research fellow, David J. Ulroan, an Inuit student from Chevak, Alaska, who came to the NMNH in 2000 on a Community Scholar Award to study with Stephen Loring, a researcher in the Arctic Studies Center in the Anthropology Department. The story of Ulroan's plaster face casting and use in the

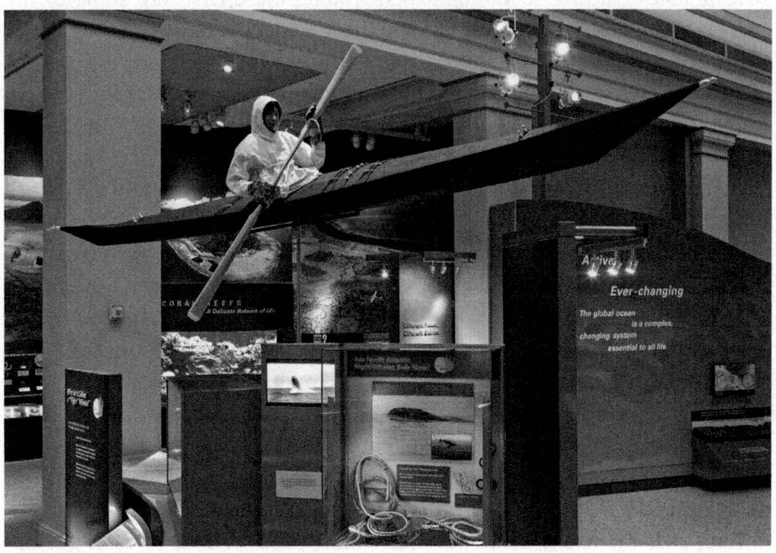


*Figure 2.1* Mannequin of David Ulroan as kayak hunter in the NMNH Sant Ocean Hall.

*Source:* Photograph from NMNH exhibits, 2020.

making of his mannequin illustrates the distance – both geographically and philosophically – between the communities that have been studied and represented in the museum, and "their" ethnographers, and where museum displays and anthropology as a discipline diverge. Ulroan's story provides a behind-the-scenes study of who is being used as models for their culture, and to ask, what does this mean in terms of the museological frameworks and practices that determine who represents who within museum galleries? This story also reveals how anthropologists have attempted a form of quid pro quo negotiation with their subjects – that is, "I will get cast if you do" – in order to get people to consent to the casting process. This, and the fact anthropologists are readily available and often amenable subjects for museum mannequins, has resulted in them being used as models for these kinds of displays. The combining of both anthropologist and anthropological subject in the museum gallery is unknown to visitors, yet these strange axioms of race/culture/science are used to present what curators and exhibit designers perceive as veracities of anthropological knowledge.

Ulroan is one of a long line of eminent Indigenous visitors to Washington DC who have been lured into or coerced by the NMNH to be cast and added to the collections. For the past 150 years, artists and NMNH technicians have made face casts of visiting Native American delegates to Washington DC, as well as Native American prisoners, Indigenous diplomats, researchers, and government boarding school students. Among these casts are some of the most important and noted Native American leaders who were travelling to DC to advocate for their people during a time in which their land and way of life were taken by military force. The practice of making face casts of Native Americans for use in the Smithsonian can be traced back to 1877 under the guidance of Spencer Fullerton Baird, the second secretary of the Smithsonian, who commissioned face casts to be made by the artist Clark Mills for use in creating mannequins for the museum galleries (Fear Segal 2013).

What role did the casts play in displaying and determining the visual signifiers and identifiers of race in museums? This growing area of research in anthropology (Manderson, 2018) includes interests in how mannequins and dioramas played a significant part in the development of the discipline as a museum-based profession (De Groff, 2012; Fitzhugh, 1997; Glass, 2009, 2010; Griffiths, 2002; Isaac, 2010, 2011, 2013; Jacknis, 1985, 2015, 2016; Sandberg, 2003; Qureshi, 2011; Wakeham, 2008). Their use also coincides with the large international expositions, such as those in London, Paris, and the US (Jacknis, 2015, 2016), with them emerging as mediators of cultural difference in the twentieth century (Griffiths, 2002). These kinds of mannequins and dioramas have also been seen as critical in exposing the tensions between how the concepts of tradition and modernity were materialized and explored via the human form in anthropology and folk museums (Sandberg, 2003).

Yet the practice of casting known and named individuals for mannequins that are subsequently used to represent human types only distinguished by their race, gender, age, etc., in the gallery is not communicated to museum visitors. The intriguing personal legacies of the models, however, provide insight into relationships between anthropologists and the people with whom they work, and more important, how these relationships and the geometries of power are negotiated. Furthermore, it is incumbent for us to ask, if an individual is used to represent a race/culture/people, what is the correlation between their anonymity and their agency? Much like the research ethics and standards provided by the Institutional Review Board – when is it appropriate to hide or share this information, who gets to decide and why?

## Past life: a history of anthropological mannequins

The origins of anthropologically-informed mannequins are intimately entwined in the colonial power structures and display genres of the "human zoos" and the exhibiting of colonized people in urban European centers (Altick, 1978; Qureshi, 2011). This practice expanded with the popularity of world fairs at the turn of the nineteenth and twentieth centuries, for which whole villages were transported and exhibited in metropolitan centers of Europe and North America. Mannequins became popular display techniques as they gave permanence, as well as animation to the cultural and physical characteristics of anthropological subjects.

The first recorded appearance of anthropologically-informed mannequins occurred in England in 1854 at Crystal Palace, when the exposition reopened with expanded exhibits and dioramas situating the fauna, flora, and people of the world according to the natural history and geographic categories of the day (Qureshi, 2011). Similar exhibits of wax mannequins of Saami people in traditional dress were created by the Swedish artist, Carl August Soderman for the 1867 International Exhibition in Paris. Soderman's work caught the attention and curiosity of viewers due to their life-like appearance: "The flesh is alive, the coloring natural; blood actually flows under the skin . . . What is most remarkable, however, is the expression on their faces . . . Certainly; they are not statues; they are living beings" (Ducuing, 1867, 123). Following the success of these life-groups, Artur Hazelius, the Swedish ethnographer and founder of the Scandinavian Ethnographic Collection, hired Soderman to produce a series for his ethnographic museum, as well as international expositions in Vienna (1873), Philadelphia (1876), Paris (1878), and Chicago (1893) (De Groff, 2012; Sandberg, 2003). By the 1870s, North American anthropologists were embarking on building similar exhibits based on their European colleagues' examples, displaying these at venues like the Philadelphia Centennial Exposition (Jacknis, 2016). George Brown Goode of the United States National Museum (which later became the building now known as the NMNH) explained that the museum was experimenting with the production of mannequins, viewing their development as an important trajectory in display techniques. Due to the high demand for anthropology exhibits for international expositions, by the 1890s the USNM had established a specialized unit that became known as the "Anthropology Laboratory" which manufactured mannequins for ten world fairs, including the Philadelphia Centennial (1876), Madrid Columbian (1893), World Columbian Exposition in Chicago (1893), Cotton States (1895), Trans-Mississippi Exposition (1898), Pan American Exposition (1901), Jamestown Exposition (1907), Alaskan-Yukon-Pacific (1909), Panama California (1915), and the Panama Pacific (1915).

In attempting to stay as faithful to life as possible, museum artists, technicians, and curators focused on duplicating morphological features, skin quality, and tone, as well as replicating hair and eyes. In discussing mannequins for the Chicago World's Fair, Goode wrote:

> Experiments are still in progress, and it is believed that figures still more truthful and life-like than any that have yet been produced will be the result. The most serious difficulty to overcome is in the treatment of the surface of the figure and their coloring. . . . Plaster of Paris has only one objection, which is the roughness of the surface. It is now believed that the smoothness and texture of the flesh can be produced by the use of some of the mineral waxes.
>
> (Goode, 1895, 55)

In emphasizing the racial characteristics of humans, curators endeavored to replicate specific physical features by using the life-casting method. We know from Baird's correspondence around the Fort Marion prisoners that he wanted the face casts to be used as the basis of mannequins. Feedback from this production process, however, showed that while the plaster casts duplicated the correct dimensions and morphology of a person's features, the life-casting method resulted in expressionless and mask-like faces: "Life masks, as ordinarily taken, convey no clear notion of the people. The faces are distorted and expressionless, the eyes are closed, and the lips compressed" (Holmes, 1903, 201). As a result, the NMNH curators elected to have face casts used as one part of the modeling process, with the museum technicians and sculptors adding animacy to the mannequin faces by opening the eyes and giving them facial expressions. To achieve what they saw as racial and gestural accuracy and to enliven these, the mannequins were constructed as composites based on face casts, photographs, and drawings of individuals, with the museum technicians producing "the physical type in each instance as accurately as the available drawings and photographs would permit" (Holmes, 1903, 201).

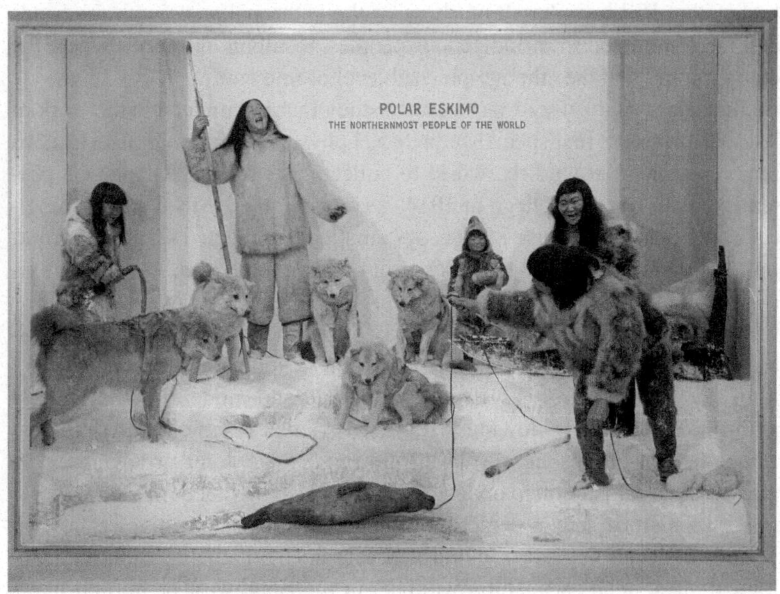


*Figure 2.2* Diorama of an Inuit family scene from the NMNH anthropology exhibit halls, which was removed in 2002.

According to William Henry Holmes – the head curator in charge of these international exposition exhibits – life-groups were the best approach for displaying the social context of each tribe or regional group: "The most important unit available for illustrating a people is the family group – the men, women, and children, with their costumes, personal adornments, and general belongings" (Holmes, 1903, 200) (Figure 2.2). As such, these groups needed not be facsimiles of race, but to show people's specific social interactions. The desire for gestural accuracy also resulted in the use of live models posing while engaged in cultural activities – such as hunting, dancing, making fire, etc. USNM anthropologists were employed or volunteered to demonstrate cultural practices they had witnessed in the field (Glass, 2009). For example, Walter Hough, Frank Hamilton Cushing, and Franz Boas posed for photographs that were used to create the mannequins' postures. Photographs depict Hough using fire-making tools, Cushing posing for the "Sioux warrior" mannequin, and Franz Boas acting out the Hamat'sa or "Cannibal Dance" of the Kwakwaka'wakw. In regard to the images of Boas, Otis Mason later wrote, "A great effort is made to expel this creature or to destroy him . . . hence the marvelous gesticulations" (Mason cited by Hinsley and

Holms, 1976). Museum technicians subsequently conjoined the mannequin bodies that had been based on those of the anthropologists with the heads and faces modeled from Indigenous peoples, resulting in hybrids where the ethnographer and the ethnographic subject became one.

The height of the use of face casts to study race culminated in the work of Aleš Hrdlička the first specialized NMNH physical anthropologist. Hrdlička sent researchers around the world to collect casts for the Panama California Exposition in San Diego in 1914. As a result, the NMNH anthropological collections now house a large, systematically collected series of portrait busts of children, adults, and elders from Native American, African American and Anglo-American communities. After their use in expositions, they were displayed at the NMNH to portray the methods of physical anthropology and, therefore, how science in the nation's capitol defined race.

In the 1940s, there was a move to update and modernize the NMNH anthropology halls. Following visitor surveys that revealed museum goers found the life-groups and displays followed a "disordered arrangement," a plan was put into action to update them. This plan included miniature dioramas with historic scenes depicting what archaeologists perceived as pivotal periods of technological or cultural developments gathered from archaeological sites, such as pueblo dwellings in the Southwest or buffalo hunts on the Plains (Ewers papers, NAA; Christiansen, 2013, 214). Ethnography curator Jack Ewers set about the task of renovation by repainting the pre-existing mannequins, using information collected by anthropologists who had employed the Von Luschan Skin Color charts – a method used for standardized identification of different skin colors. The problems of transposing Von Luschan's system directly onto the mannequins was noted: "For darker Indians, von Luschan #25–29 is too 'dead,' not enough reddish. Therefore, we suggest a reddish underpainting for many of the groups to simulate vascularity" (Ewers papers, NAA). Technicians were instructed to depict the different elements that affected skin tone, like skin darkening with age, or that women were often lighter than men and that there were different intensities of color for sections of the body more exposed to sunlight, such as the face and arms.

The renovated mannequins remained on display until 2002, when they were moved to the NMNH basement, at which point, JoAllyn Archambault, a Lakota Sioux anthropologist working for the Department of Anthropology, shared her desire to preserve them, especially as they had been linked to named individuals and to the NMNH face cast collection. She commissioned researchers to study and record their current condition, and in a memo to the Anthropology Department Collections Committee, she recommended that they "accession all manikins that survive relatively intact" as their existence was part of the historic context of the Smithsonian exhibit-making history and should, therefore, be included as part the collections of the department. In addition, she stated that "as museums begin to reflect on their own history, the artifacts of that history accordingly increase in research value" (Archambault, Dept. of Anthropology Memo, Sept. 25, 1990). By 2011, the mannequins in the best physical condition were transferred to the Physical Anthropology division of the Smithsonian collections facility in Suitland, Maryland – the Museum Support Center (MSC) – where they still reside.

## Real life? The making of ancestors today

Over the past decade, while conducting research on the NMNH mannequins, I have repeatedly been drawn to those for which there are living memories – both of their models and the stories behind their making. The story of the mannequin made of David Ulroan and his research collaborator, Stephen Loring, is one such example that enables their perspectives to be included in this project.

The creation story behind Ulroan's mannequin begins with the ongoing fieldwork conducted by Loring in Alaska. While there one summer, his host sang the praises of a young student, Ulroan, who had a deep interest in the traditional aspects to his culture. Loring subsequently explored ways for Uloran to travel to Washington DC and work on Smithsonian collections. With Loring's encouragement, Ulroan applied for and received a Community Scholar Award, which enabled him to travel to the Smithsonian, where he worked on Cup'ik artifacts from his area – the Yukon-Kuskokwim region – with his main interest being the knowledge needed to revitalize the making of traditional tools. In reflecting on his visit, he stated that, "My research enabled me to work with artifacts and crafts that I had never seen before. . . . The old tools were beautiful and I had lots of ideas about how they were made and how they were used, and I looked forward to trying them out when I got back home" (Ulroan 2000).

Ulroan also remembered his initial journey to Washington DC as "a tough challenge," since this was the first time he had traveled out of Alaska. According to Loring, when Ulroan arrived at the airport, he shared with Loring that he was both excited to come to Washington and apprehensive because:

> He had spoken to his grandmother, and she had said, "Okay, you are going away to Washington, be good and have a good time." And then her *explicit* instructions to him were, quote-un-quote, "Don't let them take your face and put it in the museum!" . . . "Don't let them put *you* in the museum!"
>
> (interview with Loring, March, 2020)

During this conversation, Loring expressed surprised at Ulroan's grandmother's concern and assured him that, "Those days are *long* gone! We don't do that anymore. You are our guest." The following morning, however, while Loring was taking Ulroan around the museum to meet colleagues, they entered the office of William Fitzhugh, the head of the Arctic Studies Center, who looked intently at Ulroan and according to Loring said: "Wow! David, nice to meet you. . . . Gee, do you think we could take a cast off your face?" Loring was stunned by this question: "I couldn't believe it! These were the *first* words out of Bill's mouth – and the *last* words out of David's mouth were of his grandmother's concern!" Fitzhugh was subsequently compelled to explain that this request was due to how he was in the midst of helping build an NMNH exhibit on Vikings, which included building a diorama with a mannequin of an Inuit man from Baffin Island, who would be seen uncovering a tool from an abandoned Norse site. According to Loring, following his explanation of Ulroan's grandmother's concerns, Fitzhugh offered to be cast at the same time to ease David's apprehensions.

As agreed upon by Fitzhugh, a cast of his face was made at the same time as Ulroan at the Smithsonian's Office of Exhibits Central (OCE). Fitzhugh's face was used for a mannequin that depicted a Viking dictating the sagas to a monk in a longhouse in Iceland. During an interview with Fitzhugh, he explained that this particular casting was not a coincidence, as he had embarked on the exhibit topic due to his interests in connecting with his own Viking ancestry. Once his mannequin had been dressed and given a beard and long hair, however, he felt less akin with it: "It did not look like me very much because they did a lot of modelling of the hair . . . I had really long hair and a beard . . . it was just the bony face structure that was mine." In reflection, he added, "You are never really too sure if you are looking at yourself" (Interview with William Fitzhugh, March 2020). In Ulroan's account of the incident, he was amused about being part of the exhibit: "My face will be traveling all over the United States for the next two years as the exhibit goes from city to city." He also shared his thoughts on the novelty of the casting process: "The best thing is that the exhibits people said they would send me a cast of my face! I am looking forward to that!" (Ulroan 2000).

The research partnership between Loring and Ulroan presents a stark paradox when experienced alongside the casting of Ulroan's physical characteristics for the museum. Ulroan noted that the highlight of his time in DC was the work that reconnected him with the cultural heritage of his community, during which he explored ways to help transmit this traditional knowledge to others in the Cup'ik community who had not been able to travel to DC:

> Stephen and I took turns filming each other while we talked about the different tools, artifacts and masks. This was so the people back home in Chevak could see what our ancestors made a long time ago. There were

> lots of things we were uncertain about, so we filmed them so that the elders back home could see the things which they would know the use for.
> (Ulroan, 2000)

Uloran also wrote of the emotional aspects of this work: "It made my spirit full of joy to see what our ancestors made, to see and carefully examine the old tools."

In interviews with curators at NMNH, they agreed the history of making face casts was fraught due to the forceful subjugation of Indigenous people under colonial regimes to submit to these intrusions, while anthropology also played a significant part in how race was portrayed to a general public via museum displays. It is understood that many anthropologists in the developmental years of the discipline used unequal power structures to coerce Indigenous people to be cast. A subject's perception and experience of this was shaped by whether they had prior knowledge of the process or had been able to give consent. Examples in the anthropological literature reveal how people who knew little of the process found it extremely frightening. In one disturbing account recorded by the Italian anthropologist, Lidio Cipriani, he pressed a Khoisan woman into the dirt and forcibly poured plaster over her face; an event which not was not only traumatic

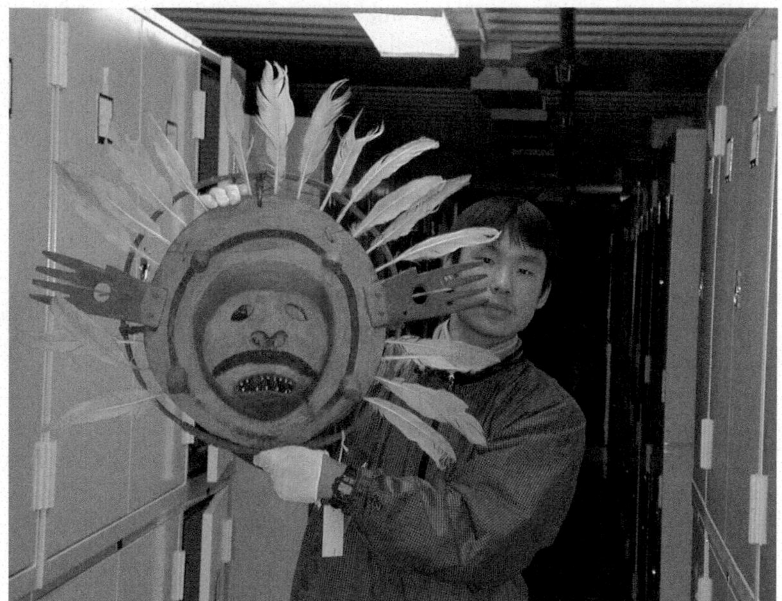

*Figure 2.3* David Ulroan working with his ancestral belongings in the NMNH Anthropology Collections.

for the woman but also created fear in her companions (Feldman, 2006, 256–257). In Anette Hoffmann's (2015) examination of casts produced by Hans Lichtenecker of people in Namibia, she recounts how one subject, Petrus Goliath, likened being cast to drowning and quotes him as saying:

> I did not hear anything, my eyes were blocked, and what was being played . . . but I could not breathe with my mouth, ears were blocked, ears were sore, sore, sore, sore, that is how it was and I sweated, wet, wet, wet, from my sweat . . . and when it was lifted from my face, I was able to get my breath back.
>
> (Hoffman, 2015, 96)

Anthropologists and museum technicians using the plaster casting method would have been aware of the extreme discomfort and dangers it presented to people. Accounts going back to the eighteenth and nineteenth centuries reveal how prominent individuals experienced the unpleasant aspects of being cast. Thomas Jefferson's casting session with the sculptor, Browere, traumatized both his family and himself (Meschutt, 1989, 11; Browere and Fox, 1940). According to Jefferson:

> [Browere] said his operation would be of about 20 minutes and less unpleasant than Houdon's method. I submitted therefore without enquiry but it was a bold experiment on his part on the health of an Octogenary . . . he suffered the plaister also to get so dry that separation became difficult & even dangerous. He was obliged to use freely the mallet & chisel to break it into pieces and get off a piece at a time. These thumps of the mallet would have been sensible almost to a loggerhead. The family became alarmed, and he confused, till I was quite exhausted, and there became real danger that the ears would separate from the head sooner than from the plaister. I now bid adieu for ever to busts & even portraits.
>
> (Jefferson quoted in Meschutt, 1989, 11)

It is also recorded that George Washington's consent to be cast was carefully and diplomatically sought, and W.W. Story, who later owned Washington's cast, claimed that Washington had felt "great unwillingness" to being cast because "the taking of a mask from life is never a pleasant operation" (Story, 1887, 144).

Gaining consent from colonized people was far less diplomatic and usually involved coercion, and in some cases was done by force. In his attempt to get Native Americans to agree, Baird stated that they had "a deeply rooted aversion to the process required. . . . The face masks from nature now in existence have, for the most part, been taken from the dead" (Baird, 1878, 201).

It is not clear which methods the sculptor Mills and prison officer Pratt used to convince the prisoners to be cast, as Mills later wrote, "The Indians were remarkably superstitious, and showed a reluctance to submit to the operation" (New York Times, 1877). Baird, however, later recalled that Mills cast Pratt to show the prisoners that the process was not harmful: "The Indians had every confidence in the statements of Captain Pratt, who had them in command, that there would be nothing detrimental to either soul or body in the process, and, indeed, he himself was first subjected to it to reassure them" (Baird, 1878, 201). While the cast of Pratt has not been found at the NMNH, the bust of the ethnomusicologist and Bureau of American Ethnology ethnologist, Frances Densmore, was discovered, most likely made in the field during the time in which Hrdlicka's assistant, Frank Micka, visited her while attempting to obtain casts of the people with which Densmore was working.

## Half life: reflections on how long power structures stay potent

The stories behind the making of current mannequins on display at NMNH have left me with much trepidation about subsequently extrapolating what they mean within the larger field of study around anthropology and the defining of race in museums. It is far easier to write about past exhibits and their problematic origins in nineteenth century racialized science, than face head-on the remaining structural inequities that are still inherent in museums, especially if one is implicated in these contemporary practices. Studying the castings of Indigenous scholars and anthropologists over time, however, has led me to ask whether the principles followed currently when making mannequins at the NMNH have in fact changed from their earlier counterparts? Or is the NMNH still following a visual framework in which "real Indians" have to be cast to make the displays "authentic"? Where are we now in terms of the power structures between anthropology, as a system of knowledge, and its subjects of study – the very people who often do not themselves participate in decision making processes in a large national museum? This endeavor, however, has not provided straightforward insights into the current defining of race within the NMNH displays. Rather it has brought me closer to experiencing firsthand how particular sub-sections of the discipline of anthropology and the museum have changed over time, yet taken different trajectories and at different paces. As a result, there are conceptual dissonances between curators, exhibit staff, community members, and also within the anthropology department itself. Ultimately, there is also a disconnect between how people think disciplinarily, and how they enact these theories within the exhibit space.

In addition, I have had to face how anthropologists express awareness amongst themselves of past problems about power inequities between scientific institutions and Indigenous communities. The negative side to the history of the discipline, however, is not shared with the public. This may be due to the prior participation of anthropology in the postcolonial, postmodern and post-paradigmatic critiques of the 1980s and 1990s that addressed anthropology's problematic origins, racist theories, and practices, including asymmetrical power relationships within representational regimes in museums (Karp and Levine, 1991; Simpson, 1996; Barringer and Flynn, 1998; Macdonald, 1998; Bunch, 2010; Lonetree, 2012; Conklin, 2013; West, 2017). Without these being unpacked publicly within the galleries of natural history and anthropology museums, however, the critique is not communicated or disseminated to the general public. Thus, while museum anthropologists understand the transformations they have undertaken to reconstruct a set of more equal and ethical anthropological practices, there are aspects of current exhibit methods that still operate according to previous positivist notions about the science of race, in which morphological typologies are privileged over social theory. This results in a split between the critiques explored within the discipline of anthropology and what is on display in the galleries.

While this dissonance can be attributed to the fact large museums, such as NMNH, have multiple divisions and sub-sets of labor and expertise so that exhibit and research departments are separate and siloed. At NMNH there is also a longstanding disjunct between the natural and social sciences, which further apportions expertise on how knowledge is manifested and evidenced in the galleries. If we go a step further into asking why this is the case, we find that the set of principles by which exhibit staff are trained are not the same as anthropology or mineral sciences, etc., with each discipline ascribing to evidentiary values that set them apart when determining how to display concepts including humankind in the museum.

This is also not helped by how, within the discipline of anthropology, there are further subdivisions between physical or biological anthropology, archaeology, and cultural anthropology. Each may follow different ideas about the extent to which the human body or material culture operate as evidence or data, and the role of Indigenous methodologies and knowledge systems in the interpretation and communication of these ideas to a wider public. As a result, there are differences in how anthropological knowledge is imagined and materialized in museum galleries, with varying degrees of trust in objects, human remains, and face casts as evidence of social science theories. While aspects of museum-based anthropology are based on the reflexive critique of the discipline, postcolonial frameworks, and Indigenous knowledge system, to others, these approaches are seen as undermining the discipline and museum as the central authority.

This results in a cacophony of voices about how race is both exhibited by the museum and experienced and or understood by visitors. Even if there are reforms and critiques in one sector of a large museum, past and ingrained practices may remain, even if their followers may be acting unconsciously and while thinking they are in fact dealing with the problem. An oft quoted phrase at the Smithsonian is "the left hand does not know what the right hand is doing," revealing that many at the institution are aware of these problems of dissonance between units. When visitors experience the galleries, however, they are not privy to these different schools of thought, and as a result, they imagine what they see as the overall institutional message. In effect, the larger the institution, the harder it is to dismantle the social inequities that have been a part of its complex structure. While this may be an obvious observation, anthropological critiques often do not in fact consider the size of the institution in their discussions around what is needed in decolonizing the museum. Having people operate simultaneously along different lines of thought, however, prevents change or at least makes it more difficult. It also should give us pause when using terms like "exhibitionary complex" or "government assemblages" which implicate museums as institutions, regimes, and governments as co-producers of power held by governments (Bennett, 1995). As shown by this exploration of mannequins at the NMNH, visitors are unaware of the debates that are taking place behind the scenes, and the fact that there is not a singular narrative in the museum on how to display race and culture. Yet we need to understand these intertwining and cross-hatchings of multiple political economies, and the discord within the societies of which museums are constituted.

In reflecting on our current social context, I am hoping that the social justice movements across the United States working to educate people more broadly about systemic racism will compel natural history and anthropology museums to move their "behind the scenes" discussions and critiques about the problematic past colonial and racist paradigms, and place these in the "front of the house." This would bring much needed opportunities to work with both diverse communities and the public, and to reach more equitable ways to disseminate the history of research on the diversity of humankind within museum galleries.

## References

Altick, Richard D. *The Shows of London*. Cambridge: Harvard University Press, 1978.

Archambault, Joallyn. Memo dated Sept. 25, 1990. Mannequin reference files. Anthropology Collections Reference Library, Museum Support Center.

Baird, Spencer Fullerton. "Catalogue of Casts Taken by Clark Mills, Esq., of the Heads of Sixty-Four Indian Prisoners of Various Western Tribes, and Held at Fort Marion, Saint Augustine, Fla., in Charge of Capt. R. H. Pratt, U.S.A." In *Proceedings of the*

*United States National Museum (v. 1 1878)*, 201. Washington, DC: Smithsonian Institution Press, 1878.

Barringer, Tim, and Tom Flynn, eds. *Colonialism and the Object: Empire, Material Culture and the Museum*. London: Psychology Press, 1998.

Bennett, Tony. *The Birth of the Museum: History, Theory, Politics*. Routledge. 1995.

Browere JHI and Fox DR. *Life Masks of Noted Americans of 1825: Exhibition, February 12 to February 24, 1940 under the sponsorship of the New York state historical association, Cooperstown, New York*. New York: M. Knoedler and Company. 1940.

Bunch, Lonnie G., III. *Call the Lost Dream Back: Essays on History, Race and Museums*. Arlington: American Alliance of Museums, 2010.

Conklin, Alice. *In the Museum of Man: Race, Anthropology, and Empire in France 1850–1950*. Ithaca, NY: Cornell University Press, 2013.

Christiansen, Erik. *Channeling the Past: Politicizing History in Postwar America*, University of Wisconsin Press, 2013.

De Groff, Daniel A. "Ethnographic Display and Political Narrative: The Salle de France of the Musee d'ethnographie du Trocadero." In *Folklore and Nationalism in Nineteenth Century Europe*, edited by Timothy Baycroft and David Hopkin. Leiden: Brill, 2012.

Ducuing, Francois, ed. *L'Exposition universelle de 1867 illustree*. Paris: Commission imperial, 1867.

Fear-Segal, J. "Plaster-Cast Indians at the National Museum." In *Indigenous Bodies: Reviewing, Relocating, Reclaiming*, edited by J. Fear-Segal and R. Tillett, 33–52. Albany: State University of New York Press, 2013.

Feldman, Jeffrey. "Contact Points: Museums and the Lost Body Problem." In *Sensible Objects: Colonialism, Museums and Material Culture*, edited by E. Edwards, C. Gosden, and R.B. Phillips, 245–268. New York: Berg, 2006.

Fitzhugh, William. "Ambassadors in Sealskins: Exhibiting Eskimos at the Smithsonian." In *Exhibiting Dilemmas: Issues of Representation at the Smithsonian*, edited by Amy Henderson and Adrienne Kaeppler. Washington, DC: Smithsonian Institution PressGlass, 1997, 2009, 2010.

Glass, Aaron. "Frozen Poses: Hamat'sa Dioramas, Recursive Representation and the Making of a Kwakkwaka'wakw Icon." In *Photography, Anthropology and History*, edited by Christopher Morton and Elizabeth Edwards, 89–118. London: Ashgate Press, 2009.

Glass, Aaron. "Review Essay: Making Mannequins Mean: Native American Representations, Postcolonial Politics, and the Limits of Semiotic Analysis." *Museum Anthropology Review* 4, no. 1 (2010): 70–84. <http://scholarworks.iu.edu/journals/index.php/mar/article/view/435>

Goode, George Browne. "Report Upon the Exhibit of the Smithsonian Institution and the United States National Museum at the Cotton States and Internal Exposition, Atlanta GA., 1895." In *Annual Report of the Board of Regents of the Smithsonian Institution*. Washington, DC: Government Printing Office, 1896.

Griffiths, Alison. *Wondrous Difference: Cinema, Anthropology and Turn-of-the-Century Visual Culture*. New York: Columbia University Press, 2002.

Hinsley, Curtis M., and Bill Holm. "A Cannibal in the National Museum: The Early Career of Franz Boas in America." *American Anthropologist* 78, no. 2 (1976): 306–316.

Hoffmann, A. "Of Storying and Storing: 'Reading' Lichtenecker's Voice Recordings." In *Re-Viewing Resistance in Namibian History*, edited by J. Silvester, 89–104. Windhoek: University of Namibia Press, 2015.

Holmes, William Henry. "The Exhibit at the Department of Anthropology, Report on the Exhibits of the U.S. National Museum at the Pan-American Exposition Buffalo, New York, 1901." In *Annual Report of the US National Museum for 1901*, 200–218. Washington, DC: Government Printing Office, 1903.

Hrdlicka, A. *A Descriptive Catalog of the Section of Physical Anthropology: Panama-California Exposition, 1915*. San Diego: National Views Company, 1914.

Isaac, Gwyneira. "Anthropology and Its Embodiments: 19th Century Museum Ethnography and the Re-Enactments of Indigenous Knowledges." *Etnofoor* 22, no. 1 (2010): 11–29.

Isaac, Gwyneira. "Whose Idea Was This? Museums, Models and the Reproduction of Indigenous Knowledges." *Current Anthropology* 52, no. 2 (2011): 211–233.

Isaac, Gwyneira. "We: Wha Goes to Washington." In *Reassembling the Collection: Ethnographic Museums and Indigenous Agency*, edited by Rodney Harrison, Sarah Byrne, and Anne Clark, 143–170. Santa Fe: School for Advanced Research Press, 2013.

Jacknis, Ira. "Franz Boas and Exhibits: On the Limitations of the Museum Method of Anthropology." In *Objects and Others: Essays on Museum and Material Culture*, edited by George Stocking, 75–111. Madison: University of Wisconsin Press, 1985.

Jacknis, Ira. "In the Field/En Plein Air: The Art of Anthropological Display at the American Museum of Natural History, 1905–30." In *The Anthropology of Expeditions: Travel, Visualities, Afterlives*, edited by Joshua A. Bell and Erin L. Hasinoff. New York: Bard Graduate Center, 2015.

Jacknis, Ira. "Refracting Images: Anthropological Display at the Chicago World's Fair 1893." In *Coming of Age in Chicago: The 1893 Word's Fair and the Coalescence of American Anthropology*, edited by Curtis M. Hinsley and David R. Wilcox, 260–336. Lincoln: University of Nebraska Press, 2016.

Karp, Ivan, and Steven D. Levine. *Exhibiting Cultures: The Poetics and Politics of Museum Display*. Washington DC: Smithsonian Press, 1991.

Lonetree, Amy. *Decolonizing Museums: Representing Native America in National and Tribal Museums*. Chapel Hill: University of North Carolina Press, 2012.

Macdonald, Sharon. *The Politics of Display: Museums, Science, Culture*. Abingdon, UK: Routledge, 1998.

Manderson, Lenore. "Humans on Show: Performance, Race and Representation: Special Issue Political Subjectivities in Times of Transformation." *Critical African Studies* 10, no. 3 (2018): 257–272.

Meschutt. D. "A Perfect Likeness: John H. I. Browere's Life Mask of Thomas Jefferson." *American Art Journal* 21, no. 4 (1989): 5–25.

New York Times, July 28. A Sculptor Among the Indians: Sixty Fur casts of Chiefs Confined at St. Augustine—The Process of Taking Them. From the Savannah News. 1877.

Qureshi, Sadiah. *Peoples on Parade: Exhibitions, Empire and Anthropology in Nineteenth-Century Britain*. Chicago: University of Chicago Press, 2011.

Sandberg, Mark B. *Living Pictures, Missing Persons: Mannequins, Museums, and Modernity*. Princeton and Oxford: Princeton University Press, 2003.

Simpson, Moira. *Making Representations: Museums in the Post-Colonial Era*. London: Routledge, 1996.

Story WW. The Mask of Washington. *Harper's Weekly*, 26 February, 144–146. 1887.

Ulroan, David. "David J. Ulroan's Smithsonian Visit, February 14–26, 2000, by David Ulroan." *Community Scholar Award Recipient, Artic Studies Newsletter*, June 2000, Number 8. <www.mnh.si.edu/arctic>

Wakeham, Pauline. *Taxidermic Signs: Reconstructing Aboriginality*. Minneapolis: University of Minnesota Press, 2008.

West, Richard W. *The Changing Presentation of the American Indian: Museums and Native Cultures*. Seattle: University of Washington Press, 2017.

# 3 Likeness and likeability

## Human remains, facial reconstructions, and identity-making in museum displays

*Minou Schraven*

As Madame Tussaud (d. 1850) knew all too well, lifelikeness sells. With its eclectic mix of lifelike wax statues, her gallery in nineteenth-century London pulled the crowds, mesmerized to stand eye to eye with the celebrities of that day. To enhance credibility of these figures, Madame insisted that they had been sculpted "after life," and that the props and dresses were as authentic as possible (Pilbeam, 2003). Today's museum visitors are equally fascinated with lifelike reconstructions of human remains in museums and heritage centers across the world.[1] Newly made reconstructions are sure to generate ample press coverage and pins in social media. After all, standing face to face with "our ancestors" is a powerful tool, whether it is by means of forensic reconstructions or by practices of historical reenactment (Agnew, 2020).

This chapter looks into the phenomenon of forensic facial and full-body reconstructions that are modeled after human remains, be it bog bodies, mummies, or skeletons. With a slight but not exclusive focus on Dutch examples, we explore the visual, rhetorical, and didactic potential of these lifelike reconstructions. A first point of interest is the indexical relationship between the lifelike reconstructions and the remains after which they are modeled. While the structure and size of the skull yields a solid base for the reconstruction of the individual's bone and muscle structures, some degree of interpretation is involved for the soft tissue areas, such as the width of the mouth and the exact shape of lips, nose, and ears (Wilkinson, 2010). Still, the very fact that the reconstructions are produced within forensic anthropology labs invests them with an aura of authenticity and authority. What does this mean for the way we view and value these reconstructions, and through them, how we interact with the very human remains on which they are modeled?

This brings us to a second point of interest: how these lifelike reconstructions allow to construct identity. By making lifelike reconstructions we somehow manage to give back to these remains what they had lost over

DOI: 10.4324/9780429260575-3

the course of time: their identity as individual human beings. This way, the reconstructions seem to appeal to a deeply ingrained need of our species to invest the remains of our dead with care (Laqueur, 2015). It is telling that remains often receive a name once their faces have been reconstructed, as if they now can reclaim their due position within our communities. Such was the case of "Ötzi," the mummy found in the Ötztal Alps in 1991; and, as we will see in more detail, of "Trijntje" and "Marcus," two skeletons found during recent archaeological excavations in the Netherlands.[2] As we will see in greater detail for Lindow Man (British Museum, 1985) and Yde Girl (Drents Museum, Assen, 1994), local communities have strongly responded to their lifelike reconstructions, recognizing them as "one of their own." Today's advanced forensic research methods, such as the extraction of ancient DNA, open up entirely new avenues for the research of mortal remains. Besides reconstructing their facial likeness, we can today learn about their genetic makeup, and identify the geographical locations where they spent certain parts of their lives. In the final part of this chapter, we will explore the impact of these new scientific methods, and their implications for identification with human remains and their reconstructions.

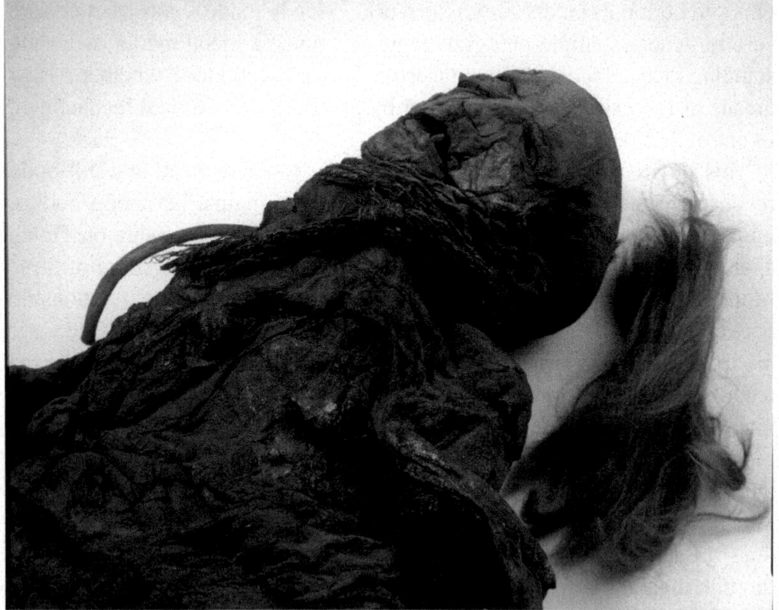

*Figure 3.1* Remains of female bog body ("Yde Girl"), dated between 54 BCE and 128 CE; retrieved in 1897 (Drents Museum, Assen).

Photo: JAV Studio's, with permission.

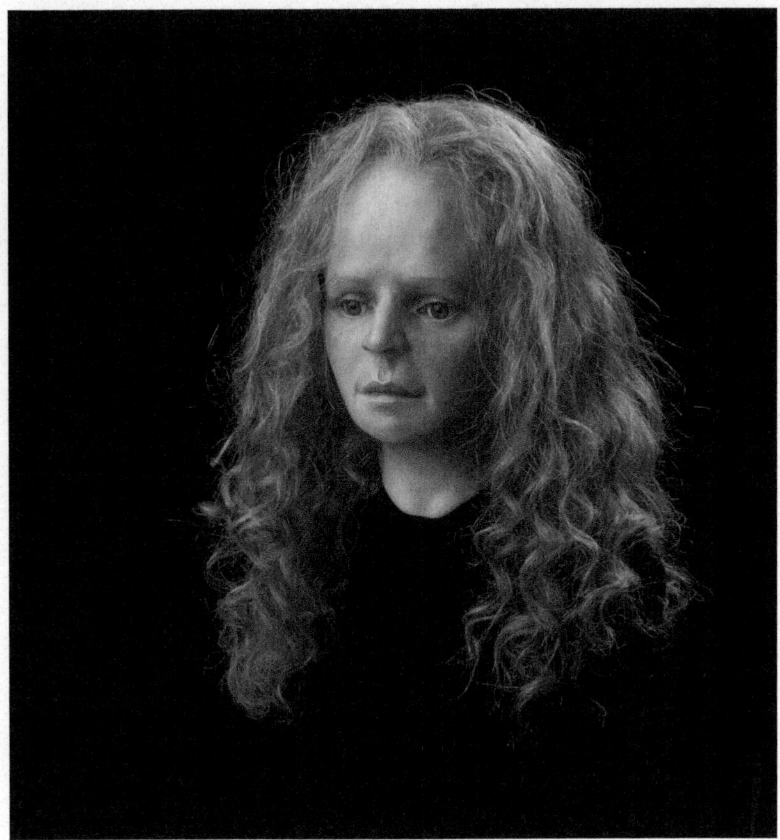

*Figure 3.2* Facial reconstruction of "Yde Girl", made in 1994 by Richard Neave (Drents Museum, Assen).

Photo: JAV Studio's, with permission.

## Bog faces reconstructed: Lindow Man and Yde Girl

The first facial reconstruction of human remains in the Netherlands was made in 1994 for a body belonging to a – as we know now – 16-year-old girl, who died between circa 54 BCE and 128 CE (Figure 3.1). Her body had been found in a relatively small bog in 1879, south of the modern-day village Yde in the Northern Netherlands, hence her name "Yde Girl." At the time of her death, large parts of Northern Europe were covered with wetlands: sites of great ritual significance for the local communities. Due to their particular chemical composition, bogs are excellent in preserving organic material such as wood, textiles, and soft tissues of bodies (Ravn,

2010; Van Beek, Candel, and Quick, 2019). After 2,000 years in the peat, her skin had turned all brown and leather like, and her long blonde hair had assumed a bright red color. Half of her scalp had been shaven off, probably as part of the ritual in which she had been strangled: the woolen band was still tightly wrapped around her neck.[3] Her body was eventually taken to the Provincial Museum of Antiquities in Assen, where it was left to dry out: the only preservation method known at the time.[4]

It would take until the late 1980s until this and other bog bodies from the collection of the Drents Museum were subjected to systematic research. This way, the age, sex, and length (just 1.40 meters) of Yde Girl could finally be determined. Examination of her skeleton also revealed that she had suffered from a mild form of scoliosis, which caused her to slope while walking: this must have made her stand out in her community. While the injuries to her skull probably had been inflicted by the peat-cutters who found her, the cause of death was indeed a deep wound round her neck, caused by "garroting with tightening occurring at the position of the knot on the left side" (Parg and Neave, 168; Van der Sanden, 1996). She also had a deep stab wound at the base of her throat.

Given that Yde Girl's skull had been preserved intact, she was the ideal candidate for a facial reconstruction (Groen and Souwer, 2014). For this reconstruction, curator Wijnand Van den Sanden turned to medical artist Richard Neave and archaeologist John Prag at Manchester University. Just nine years earlier, they had made a facial reconstruction of a male bog body that had been discovered in Lindow Moss, in the greater Manchester area, in August 1984. The remains of Lindow Man, consisting of the upper body and the left leg, were transferred to the British Museum in London for preservation and analysis according to the latest insights. The curators decided to opt for freeze drying to prevent shrinkage of the body (Joy, 2010).

Heralded as the archaeological discovery of the century, Lindow Man, or "Pete Marsh" as he was called in the popular press, proved to be an instant sensation. In April 1985, over 10 million people tuned in for a BBC documentary chronicling the conservation process and the first results of research into the cause of death and into the contents of his stomach.[5] Yet despite this impressive amount of data, it was still quite a step to imagine that the disfigured and discolored remains had once belonged to a breathing human being. Hence the decision of the British Museum to commission a facial reconstruction of the bog body from Neave and Prag.[6] As the actual bones of the skull of Lindow Man were inaccessible, Neave and his team based themselves on indirect data retrieved from photographs and computerized tomographic (CT) scans, which are rather crude methods when compared to the advanced techniques of today. The facial reconstruction of Lindow Man was given clear eyes and dark hair, as befitting his supposed Celtic descent.[7]

The remains of Lindow Man and his facial reconstruction were presented to the public the following year in the exhibition "Archaeology in Britain." When Lindow Man was loaned for six months to the Manchester Museum, it attracted a massive 2,000 visitors a day. Outraged that the bodily remains eventually would be returned to London, Brenda O'Brian started a campaign to keep the body in the Manchester region. She wrote the lyrics for the campaign song "Lindow Man, We Want You Back Again," performed by children of Lindow Primary School. In the "world's first video petition," shots of singing children wearing their blue campaign T-shirts were alternated with images of the group walking in the Lindow countryside dressed as young Celts (O'Brian, 2010). O'Brian's petition got the backing of many members of Parliament of the North-West. Local and national newspapers featured headlines, such as "Pete Should Stay in the North" and "Tug-of-war Over the Body in the Bog." Clearly, the ancient body fueled sentiments about the North-South divide between the region of Manchester and a capital city that "has it all" (Joy, 2010; Sitch, 2010).[8]

Given the vivid response to Lindow Man, expectations ran high in Drenthe, now that Neave and Prag started to work on the facial reconstruction of Yde Girl. But this proved far more challenging than anticipated. Whereas the remains of Lindow Man had been professionally excavated and preserved according to the latest insights, those of Yde Girl had been left to dry out. As a consequence, her skull had shrunk to half its original size. Nonetheless, Neave's team managed to make a facial reconstruction of the adolescent girl, with a rather high forehead and striking blond curls (Prag and Neave, 1997).[9] Presented in 1994, the facial reconstruction of Yde Girl was an instant sensation (Figure 3.2). Science had provided a rather unattractive, discolored, and desiccated bog body with the face of a healthy young girl. In the general media frenzy of that summer, the Drents Museum organized a Miss Bog Body pageant to find the girl that looked most like the reconstruction (*De Telegraaf*, 1994). That same summer, the newly opened archaeological theme park *Archeon* in Alphen aan den Rijn staged a drama about the sacrifice of Yde Girl. A baker from the Yde area started to sell biscuits with the head of Yde Girl, and there was a local initiative to honor her with a monument. A reader of the national newspaper *Trouw* took offense: in a letter to the editor, he asked what the achievements of Yde girl were exactly, to merit such consideration.[10] Twenty-five years later, the enthusiasm for Yde Girl is still undiminished, judging from the unrelenting production of children's books, television coverage, and theater plays.[11] Between 2002 and 2004, the body and facial reconstruction traveled the world along with six other bog bodies in the exhibition *The Mysterious Bog People: Ritual and Sacrifice in Ancient Europe*, organized by museums in the Netherlands, Germany, and Canada.[12]

This unwavering interest in Yde Girl stands in stark contrast with another facial reconstruction produced by Neave's team in about the same period. In 1998, the Rijksmuseum van Oudheden in Leiden commissioned a facial reconstruction of the mummy of Sensaos (d. 119 CE), daughter of the governor of Thebes. The girl was 16 years old when she died, the same age as the Yde Girl. Non-intrusive CT-scans produced a three-dimensional copy of the skull that served as basis for the facial reconstruction. Although the museum has displayed the reconstruction for about a decade, Sensaos never won the hearts of the public like Yde Girl did. Apparently, there needs to be a strong local connection with the finding place of the human remains to fully nurture the idea that the body could indeed have been "one of us."

## Bog people preserved: Tollund Man and Grauballe Man

Due to the weight of the peat, and in case of Yde Girl, because of shrinkage, the actual faces of Lindow Man and Yde Girl had been disfigured beyond

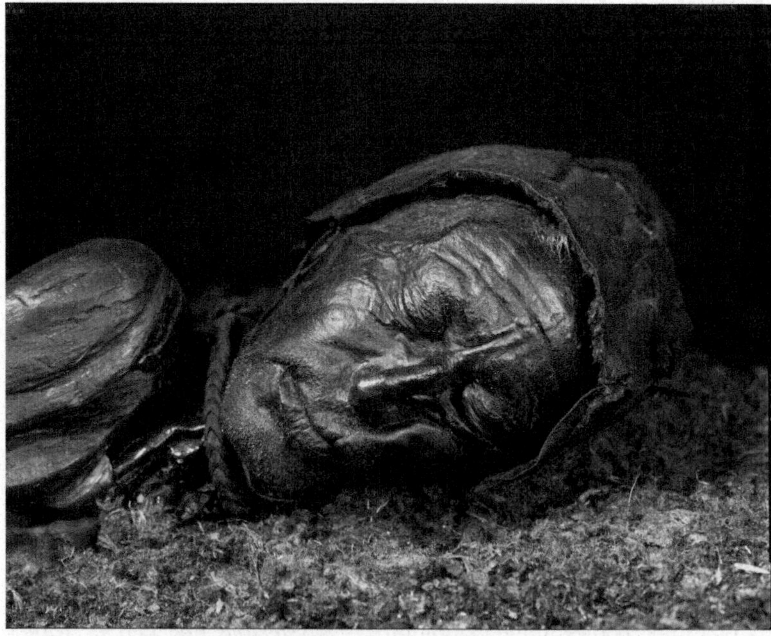

*Figure 3.3* Head of male bog body ("Tollund Man"), dated ca 400 BCE; retrieved in 1950 (Silkeborg Museum, Denmark).

recognition. It was the merit of the facial reconstructions that the larger public could appreciate the human dimension of these remains. But decades before the forensic scientific method used by Neave and his team had been perfected, two sensationally well-preserved bog bodies found in Denmark had offered audiences the chance to stand face to face with men from a distant past: Tollund Man (dated c. 400 BCE), found in 1950, and Grauballe Man (dated c. 290 BCE) found in 1952.[13] Of the two, Tollund Man is the most intact and, because of its tranquil expression, arguably the most evocative of all bog bodies that have come to us (Figure 3.3).[14]

Peacefully curled up in the peat, yet with a noose still round his neck, his friendly face with his delicate wrinkles and day-old beard stubble has touched and inspired generations of museum visitors, including Irish poet and Nobel laureate Seamus Heaney and German artist Joseph Beuys (Sanders, 2009). Making headlines in newspapers across the world, the discovery of these two bodies marked the coming of age of prehistoric archaeology of Northwestern Europe. Compared to the long and venerable tradition of Mediterranean archaeology, interest in prehistoric cultures north of the Alps had been of a much more recent date. Because of a lack of written records compared to the classical Mediterranean world, the young discipline was in need of its own methodology. To complicate matters, it also needed to rid itself from decades of pseudo-scientific research of Nazi ideologists into Northern European civilizations.

In 1935, Heinrich Himmler had founded a special research division within the SS, the *Ahnenerbe*, in order to underpin the supposed superiority of the Aryan race by means of archaeological research and ethnographic expeditions (Pringle, 2006). By 1939, the *Ahnenerbe* research center was located in Berlin's most prestigious neighborhood and had a staff of 137 senior scholars and scientists.[15] Brought up with the Norse sagas and the *Nibelungenlied*, the young Heinrich Himmler had been captivated by Tacitus' *Germania* (1st century CE). In a diary entry of September 1924, Himmler stated that *Germania* offered "a wonderful portrait of how high, pure and capable our ancestors were. This is how we will become again, or at least part of us will" (Pringle, 2006, 15–18). With *Germania*, Tacitus wanted to provide his readers with an antidote to the decadence and opulence he perceived in Roman society. This aspect was lost on German nationalists like Himmler, who took the unbridled praise of the courage and valor of the ancient tribes living north of the rivers Rhine and Danube at face value.

As these Northern tribes had not left written records, generations of scholars had mined *Germania* for information about their religious customs and practices. Tacitus had for instance written about the custom to drown slaves in a sacred lake (*Germania*, XL). In another passage (*Germania*, XII), Tacitus mentioned *corpores infames*, whose punishment consisted in being pinned down in the bog (Green, 1998). With these passages in hand, Johanna Mestor (d. 1909), professor in German prehistoric archaeology, identified the bodies found in bogs as those of executed criminals and slaves.[16] Taking this interpretation one step further, Karl-August Eckhardt (d. 1979), university professor in Germanic law, SS *Sturmbahnführer* and personal friend of Himmler, identified the *corpores infames* with deviant members of Germanic society, which he classified as adulterers, traitors, and homosexuals (Eckhardt, 1937, 20).[17] At the time, Nazi officials considered homosexuality a contagious social disease that posed a serious threat to discipline and moral rectitude within their masculinist organizations, such as the SS and the *Hitlerjugend* (Himmler, 1937; Oosterhuis, 1991).

In a speech for high officials of the SS about the "pestilence" of homosexuality, Heinrich Himmler referred to the interpretation of bog bodies as *corpores infames*. He called for vigilance, referring to the way Germanic tribes had handled transgressions in the past: "They [90% of all bog bodies excavated by the 'learned professors' were homosexuals, according to Himmler] had to be removed, just when we pull out nettles, stack them, and burn them. It was not a question of revenge, but simply that they had to be done away with. That is how our ancestors did it" (Sanders, 2009, 61–62). This is not to say that alternative interpretations of bog bodies could not exist: when an intact bog body of a young girl was found in July 1939 in Dröbnitz (the actual Drwęck in Poland), a German newspaper described her as a "Germanic beauty," rather than a deviant member of society (Sanders, 2009, 63; Van der Sanden, 1996, 89).[18]

## Bog bodies: from *corpores infames* to sacrificial victims and fallen kings

With the fall of Nazi Germany, the interpretation of the *corpores infames* lost its relevance and appeal. Along with the discovery of Tollund Man and Grauballe Man in the early 1950s, archaeologists convincingly connected the bodies to other categories of objects that had been ritually deposited in the bogs.[19] The new interpretation as sacrificial victims made it far easier for the public to identify with them (Asingh, 2007; Joy 2010, 13). As Karen Sanders has observed, newspapers of the time routinely described Tollund Man and Grauballe Man as having "aristocratic facial features," the very opposite of slaves or criminals.

When the two bog bodies were found in the early 1950s, scientific research in their preservation was still in its infancy. When the body of Tollund Man was sent over to the National Museum in Copenhagen, it was decided to preserve only its head, right foot, and thumb.[20] The rest of Tollund Man's body was eventually disposed of, partly because a corpse like this was judged "too macabre" to be displayed (Joy, 2010, 13; Sanders, 2009, 26–29).[21] But times were changing fast. When Grauballe Man was discovered in 1952, Danish archaeologist Peter Vilhelm (Glob) was determined to preserve the entire body and display it as such. Before embarking on the two-year long process of preservation, Glob also insisted to put the body on display for ten days, to the chagrin of the curators of the Prehistoric Museum in Aarhus. It proved to be a stroke of genius: over 18,000 people queued long hours to catch a glimpse of the body, displayed in a glass casket and constantly watered down to keep moisture levels intact. This way, the two bog bodies of Tollund Man and Grauballe Man nestled themselves deeply in the consciousness of the Danish public (Asingh, 2007, 14–50; Joy, 2010, 13).

While pollen analysis quite early on allowed scientists to date the body of Grauballe Man to 500 BCE, during the viewing period local farmers claimed to recognize the body as "Red Christian," a peat-cutter who had disappeared from the scene after a night's drinking in 1887. The controversy made headlines in the national newspapers, dividing inhabitants of Jutland into two camps: those in favor and those skeptical about science. The issue was settled with the outcome of carbon-14 tests, among the first executed outside the US, that irrefutably dated the body of Grauballe Man to the Iron Age (Glob, 2009, 59–62; Asingh, 2007, 29–31).

In the last decades, the interpretation of bog bodies as sacrificial victims has been refined. Besides offerings to fertility gods, human sacrifice may just as well have occurred in connection with military victories, thanksgiving, and divination rituals.[22] In absence of written evidence, we should be wary of generalizations and acknowledge that the Northern European bog bodies come from very distinct time periods and cultures. This much is evident from a recent interpretation of a small subset of Irish bog bodies dating from the Iron Age. All four bodies are of young men in their late twenties, who suffered violent deaths and were buried along the ancient boundaries of Irish kingdoms. Therefore, Eamonn Kelly of the National Archaeological Museum in Dublin identifies them with local kings who were ritually sacrificed for having failed to provide food and safety to their subjects. This interpretation is the guiding principle in the permanent *Kingship and Sacrifice* exhibit in the Dublin museum, as it opened in 2006 (Kelly, 2012, 232–240).

Each of the bodies is displayed behind glass in its own individual niche, with a simple bench where the museum visitor can sit down to engage with the human remains. Information boards and videos are deliberately presented outside of these niches. Besides giving information about the excavation and analysis of the remains, the presentation places emphasis on the specific locations where they were found. To support their identification as fallen kings, certain markers of high social status are singled out, such as the absence of calluses on the hands, and the resin found in the hair of Clonycavan Man (dated between 392 and 201 BCE): resin was a costly import from Southern France or Spain. Close examination of the body of Old Croghan Man (dated between 362 and 175 BCE) has revealed that his nipples had been cut. Kelly connects this to a passage in St. Patrick's writings, where suckling of the nipples of a king is mentioned as a sign of submission. Now that the nipples are mutilated, this ritual act is no longer possible, once more enforcing the interpretation of the body as that of a fallen king. The interpretation fits well with the narrative of a self-conscious and independent Irish nation (Comer, 2015, 129–134).

In 2007, a facial reconstruction was made of Clonycavan Man, that is currently on display within the *Kingship and Sacrifice* exhibition. Produced by Caroline Wilkinson, a British physical anthropologist, special attention has been given to the stubble of a goatee on the chin, and the remarkable elevated hairstyle of Clonycavan man, with its use of a resin-based hair gel (Wilkinson, 2010).

## Full-body lifelike reconstructions in the Netherlands: "Trijntje"

After the success of the facial reconstructions made after several bog bodies and Egyptian mummies, it did not take long until the first full body reconstruction was made. The first time that this happened in the Netherlands was for a female skeleton that had been excavated in 1997. Dated to c. 5500 BCE, the body is to date the oldest complete skeleton found in the Netherlands and Belgium. The excavation took place during the preparations of one of the most ambitious and costly infrastructure projects in recent Dutch history, the *Betuwe-route*. Constructed between 1998 and 2007, this 160-km freight railway between Rotterdam and the German border cuts right through the rural Betuwe, a landscape mentioned in Julius Caesar's *De Bello Gallico*. After protests from environmentalists and local communities, just one of its three branches was realized, and that at a cost of 4.7 billion euro, more than double the original estimate.

Just a few months into the actual fieldwork, in December 1997, archaeologists came across a sensational find, a complete female skeleton dating from the Stone Age. The skeleton was found at a depth of six meters near Hardinxveld-Giessenbeek, north of Dordrecht. Aged between 40 and 60 years old, the woman had been living in a Stone Age community of fishers and hunters. When it was presented to the international press, the skeleton was given the name "Trijntje" ["train-cha"]: a traditional Dutch name, with a pun to the railway construction. The find was a huge and much-needed boost for the complex *Betuwe-route* project, amidst its many delays, spiraling costs, and a much-divided public opinion (Verhart, 2001).

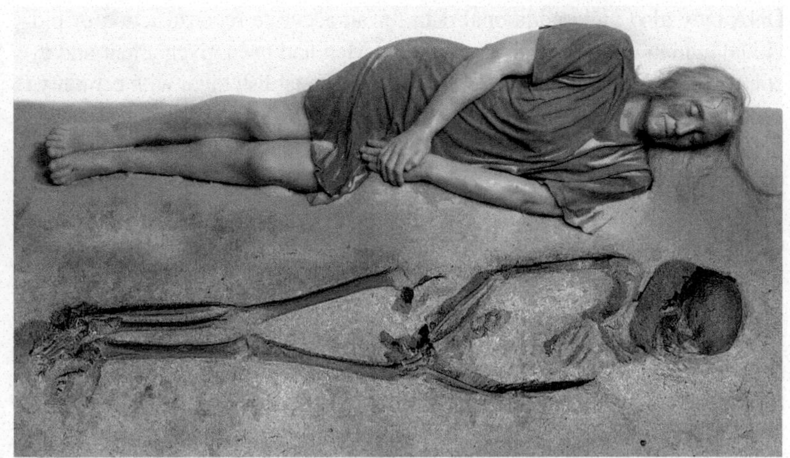

*Figure 3.4* Full body reconstruction of "Trijntje" skeleton, ca 7500 BCE, made in 2001 by Maja d'Hollosy.

Photo: Rijksmuseum van Oudheden, Leiden.

To mark the completion of archaeological excavations along the *Betuwe-route*, an exhibition of its most remarkable finds traveled along the itinerary in 2001. Besides a woolly rhinoceros and a wooden kanoo (the second-oldest in the world), the skeleton of "Trijntje" was one of the eye-catchers. For this occasion, a full-body reconstruction of the skeleton was commissioned from Amsterdam-based physical anthropologist Maya d'Hollosy: one of her first reconstruction projects (Figure 3.4).[23] The reconstruction presents a middle-aged woman with long grey hair dressed in a long shirt. The woman lays on her side with her hands clasped, the position in which the skeleton had been found. Having been displayed at the Rijksmuseum van Oudheden in Leiden for about a decade, the reconstruction of "Trijntje" is currently in a small museum near the location where her skeleton was found.[24]

## Ancient DNA: "Marcus" van Eindhoven and the primordial Vlaardinger

Back in 1994, the public had been startled by the lifelikeness of the facial reconstruction of Yde Girl, and they were thrilled to spot her look-a-like in the Miss Bog Body pageant. Since then, far more refined research and scanning methods have been developed to study ancient human remains. An important step was the mapping of human DNA in the Human Genome Project (1990–2003). The extraction of ancient DNA had immense implications for our knowledge of human migration patterns. Information retrieved from ancient DNA may also yield additional data for an accurate reconstruction of individual human remains. Whereas Lindow Man had been given a hair and eye color based on best guess, ancient DNA could establish them with certainty.[25]

The first time that Dutch scientists managed to extract ancient DNA was in 2002, during the examination of a medieval skeleton of a child. The skeleton had been found earlier that year during an excavation in Eindhoven, in front of the present-day church of St. Catherine (Arts, 2002, 22–53). The bones of the child were brittle and had therefore not been preserved. The skull was in a much better state, permitting the extraction of DNA from the teeth. This way, it could be established that the skeleton had belonged to a boy about 10 years old. The child must have been chronically ill, given that his teeth were covered with ridges. The location of burial, right in front of the high altar of the medieval church, indicated that his parents must have been members of the local aristocracy (Arts, 2002, 54–78). Near the boy's jaw, archaeologists found a small, pierced silver coin of 20 millimeter in diameter. It was identified as a Venetian *grosso*, with the portrait of St. Mark, the patron of Venice. Given that the coin was heavily worn, it must have had special significance for the boy's family, hence the decision to name him "Marcus" van Eindhoven. Maja d'Hollosy was commissioned to make a facial reconstruction of the skull, that was placed on a full-body reconstruction. It was presented in 2002 during the exhibition *Marcus en Mo*, comparing the lives and times of Marcus to those of Mo, an imaginary teenager living in today's Eindhoven (Arts, 8–19).

It is one thing to retrieve ancient DNA from old human remains, but quite another to look for a match in the current population. This was the driving idea for the quest for the primordial inhabitant of Vlaardingen in 2007. During excavations near the Grote Kerk of Vlaardingen, about forty-nine skeletons had been found. They could be dated to the first half of the eleventh century. The archaeological department of the City of Vlaardingen commissioned facial reconstructions for six of these skulls from Maja d'Hollosy. Given that the molars had yielded ancient DNA, the city archaeologist came up with the idea to look for a match within the current population. Citizens with a strong Vlaardingen pedigree, for instance bearing typical surnames of the area, such as Buttgen, Drop, and Brobbel, were invited to donate some DNA. Out of 180 hopefuls, eighty-eight persons were selected for further research. During a festive event in July 2007, a retired dentist from Rotterdam was officially proclaimed to be a relation to the primordial Vlaardinger. As was to be expected, the dentist proudly posed for pictures together with the facial reconstruction of his supposed "ancestor" (Groen and Ridder, 2007; De Rooij, 2012).

With ever advancing scanning techniques and visualization methods, the investigation of ancient human bodies yields spectacular results. An important step in this regard was the traveling exhibition *Mummy: The Inside Story* of the British Museum in 2004, that offered visitors a three-dimensional immersive experience within the mummy of Egyptian priest Nesperennub, who lived c. 800 BCE in Thebes (Hopkin, 2004). In 2014, this idea was taken to the next level with the exhibition *Ancient Lives, New Discoveries*, held at the British Museum. Three dimensional visualizations of high resolution CT-scans allowed visitors to virtually explore the bodies of eight mummies of the collection, including their most intimate medical histories (Taylor, 2014). Likewise, the Museon in The Hague presented the *Cold Case* exhibition in 2015, where the public could engage with the latest scientific methods to study human remains. Apart from DNA, special attention was given to strontium isotope analysis, that allows to retrace geographical locations where an individual has stayed during specific periods of his or her life (Levine, 2017).

This advanced research method has been very successful in the case of the Haraldskjaer Woman, a female bog body (dated around 490 BCE), found in Jutland, northern Denmark, in 1835.[26] Strontium isotope research on a small piece of tooth enamel established that the woman had spent her childhood in Jutland. But in order to find out what had happened to her in later years, Karin Margarita Frei of the National Museum of Denmark developed a method for extracting strontium from the woman's 50 centimeter-long hair. The results were spectacular: analysis of the isotopes proved that the woman had been traveling extensively in the months before she died, probably to Central Germany or the United Kingdom. Frei examined a similar case, that of the Huldremose Woman (dated between 160 BCE and 340 CE), also found in a bog in Jutland and now at the National Museum of Denmark. Again, strontium isotope analysis showed that the woman had traveled extensively towards the very end of her life. According to Frei, it may mean that these travels, perhaps to distant sanctuaries, were an integral part of the ritual of sacrifice (Levine, 2017).

Besides these scientific methods, animation techniques now allow for virtual reconstructions of human remains, such as that of Tollund Man, recently produced by Paris-based Virtualforensic. Likewise, the traveling exhibition *The Mysterious Bog People: Ritual and Sacrifice in Ancient Europe* included an animated virtual reconstruction of Yde Girl, who invited the museum visitors to explore her life and times.

New scientific research methods, like strontium isotope analysis and powerful CT scans, yield new data about human remains of distant pasts, complementing their biographies and pathologies in spectacular ways. Previous interpretations about their lives and deaths need to be constantly reevaluated and adjusted, as we come to terms with the very individuality of these remains, and the realization that the interpretations of their remains are firmly rooted in the demands and needs of our own time.

## Notes

1 The list of forensic reconstructions is vast and growing day by day, from the body of Ötzi (South Tyrol Museum of Archaeology, 2011, by Adrie and Alfons Kennis), to the head of King Richard III (d. 1485) in Leicester (2013, made by Caroline Wilkinson), and "Cheddar Man," the facial reconstruction based on a 10,000-year-old skeleton in the collection of the Natural History Museum in London (2013, Adrie and Alfons Kennis). The "Evolution Stairs" in the Moesgaard Museum, near Aarhus, Denmark, displays seven anatomically correct reconstructions of early *hominins*, from "Lucy" found in Ethiopia to the Koelbjerg Man, the oldest skeleton of Denmark (Price, 2015).

2 Following Laqueur, we could categorize names as "Tollund Man," "Yde Girl," and "Ötzi" as "space deixes": indexical names that depend on a geographical location; Laqueuer (2015, 365) uses this term for names on gravestones.

3 Today, the reddened hair is displayed alongside the body: in the first week after the discovery of the body, inhabitants of the area had taken the hair and most of the teeth as curiosities; they were eventually reunited to the body in the museum.

4 Archival records demonstrate that until well into the nineteenth century, bog bodies were habitually reburied in churchyards (Ravn, 2010).

5 The award-winning Q.E.D. science documentary series aired during the 1980s and 1990s (Joy, 2010, 14).

6 As part of the "Manchester Mummy Team," Neave and Prag had already produced several facial reconstructions of Egyptian mummies in the Manchester Museum. The British Museum no longer displays the facial reconstruction of Lindow Man: its inventory number is 1984,1002.1 (Prag and Neave, 1997, 157–171).

7 Nowadays, ancient DNA can yield information such as the color of skin, hair, and eyes, see note 25.

8 Despite the restitution campaign, Lindow Man's body remained in London. It was loaned several times to the Manchester Museum, most recently in 2008 for the exhibition *Lindow Man: A Bog Body Mystery*. During the accompanying conference "Respect for Ancient British Human Remains: Philosophy and Practice," professionals and academics exchanged best practices about the display and care of human remains in museum collections. Back in the 1980s, no museum curator or archaeologist had endorsed O'Brian's restitution campaign.

9 The decision to depict the girl in good health, before she met her violent death, certainly helped the public to identify with the reconstruction. D'Hollosy's reconstruction of "Hermen of Zwolle," a skeleton of a late medieval murder victim found in 2010 in Zwolle, depicts the body shortly after his violent death, with a wound at the head. The body used to be displayed in the Broerenkerk in Zwolle. http://skullpting.eu/site/en/projects/late-middle-ages/zwolse-harry/

10 The monument in Yde was never realized; the provincial authorities placed, however, an informative board on the location where the body of Yde Girl was found, illustrated with images of both the facial reconstruction and the bog body (*Trouw*, Letter to the Editor, June 28, 1994).

11 During the summer of 2018, the open-air theater near Yde presented a local production in which Yde Girl was presented as a local heroine, who had volunteered to be sacrificed to the gods to safeguard her community from the invading Romans. The play was written by Peter Tuinman.

12 Organizing museums were the Drents Museum in Assen, the Niedersächsisches Landesmuseum in Hannover, the Canadian Museum of Civilization of Gatineau, and the Glenbow Museum of Calgary. See Heather Gill-Robinson, "Bog Bodies on Display," *Journal of Wetland Archaeology* 4 (2004): 111–116, about the controversy that the display of bog bodies caused in Canada.

13 Grauballe Man is on display in Moesgaard Museum, 10 km from Aarhus, Denmark. In 2001, the body was subjected to extensive research and a facial reconstruction was made by Caroline Wilkinson. Pauline Asingh and Niels Lynnerup, eds., *Grauballe Man: An Iron Age Bog Body Revisited* (Jutland Archaeological Society, 2007).

14 The body of Tollund Man is now on display in Museum Silkeborg, Denmark. When the remains were discovered, it was decided to preserve just the head and a finger: the rest of the partly decomposed body was eventually disposed of. In 1986, a reconstruction of the missing parts of the body was made, based on photographs taken in the 1950s. The museum website has a video with the digital facial reconstruction of Tollund Man in movement: www.museumsilkeborg.dk/tollundmand-reconstruction.

15 Pringle makes clear that the merciless "purging" of the SS death squads in Southern Russia and the Crimea went hand in hand with efforts of *Ahnenerbe* archaeologists to locate early Gothic settlements that would justify the Nazi-German invasion of this territory (Pringle, 2006, 235).

16 As Ravn (2010) points out, Fridrich Ahrends (d. 1861) was the first to connect the bog bodies in East Friesland and Harlingerland to Tacitus. F. Ahrends, *Erdbeschreibung des Fürstentums Ostfriesland und des Harlingerlandes* (Emden, 1824), p. 164ss., referred to the Marx-Etzel bog body (dated to c. 100 CE), which had been found in 1817.

17 *Das Scharze Korps* was the official weekly newspaper of the SS.

18 The body was destroyed towards the end of the WWII.

19 Ravn (2010, 116), mentions that Danish archaeologist Elise Thorvildsen (d. 1998) was the first to make this connection. This approach still remains relevant for present-day research, such as David Fontijn's research project into "Economies of Destruction. The Emergence of Metalwork Disposition during the Bronze Age in Northwest Europe," that currently runs at Leiden University.

20 Although the head shrunk about 12% in the conservation process, it has retained its exceptionally detailed facial features.

21 Joy (2010, 13) and Sanders (2009, 26–29). The body that we see now in the museum in Silkeborg is a reconstruction made in 1985 after photographs taken during the conservation process.

22 Ravn p. 16; W. Van den Sanden, "Bog Bodies: Underwater Burials, Sacrifices, and Executions," in Francesco Menotti and Aidan O'Sullivan (eds.), *The Oxford Handbook of Wetland Archaeology* (Oxford: Oxford University Press, 2012), pp. 401–416.

23 See Maja d'Hollosy's website for a full catalogue of her work. http://skullpting.eu/site/en/

24 The female skeleton is currently on display in Openluchtmuseum Arnhem, as part of the "Canon van Nederland"; the reconstruction of her body is displayed in local museum De Gouden Knop in Hardinxveld-Giessendam, near Dordrecht.

25 Following the retrieval of the skeleton of King Richard III of England underneath a Leicester carpark in 2012, Caroline Wilkinson was commissioned to produce a facial reconstruction based on the skull. Initially, the reconstruction

was given dark hair, but once ancient DNA pointed out that the king actually had been blond, the reconstruction was adjusted accordingly: www.culture24.org.uk/history-and-heritage/royal-history/art52050-head-of-richard-third-reconstructed-in-four-hour-operation-based-on-dna-test-results

26 For the fascinating but false identification of these remains as Queen Grunhild of Norway (d. 970), see Karen Sanders, "A Portal through Time: Queen Gunhild," *Scandinavian Studies* 81, no. 1 (2009): 1–46.

## Bibliography


Agnew, Vanessa, Jonathan Lamb, and Juliane Tomann, eds. *The Routledge Handbook of Reenactment Studies: Key Terms in the Field*. London: Routledge, 2020.

Arts, Nico. *Marcus van Eindhoven. Een archeologische biografie van een middeleeuws kind*. Utrecht: Matrijs, 2002.

Asingh, Pauline. "'The Man in the Bog' and Helle Strehle: 'The Conservation of Grauballe Man'." In *Grauballe Man: An Iron Age Bog Body Revisited*, edited by Pauline Asingh and Niels Lynnerup. Højbjerg / Moesgård: Jutland Archaeological Society Publications, 2007.

Comer, Margaret. "Ancient Bodies, Modern Ideologies: Bog Bodies and Identity in Denmark and Ireland." In *Identity and Heritage: Contemporary Challenges*, 129–134. Turnhout: Brepols, 2015.

de Rooij, Martine. "Oer-Vlaardinger and Oer-Vlaardinger: Genetica in de Stad." Unpublished MA thesis in Sociology, The Netherlands: University of Amsterdam, 2012.

*De Telegraaf*. "Monique gekozen tot Miss Veenlijk," June 20, 1994.

Eckhardt, K.A. "Widernatürliche Unzucht is todeswürdig." *Das Schwarze Korps* 20 (1937).

Glob, Peter Vilhelm. *The Bog People: Iron-Age Man Preserved*. New York: Review Book Classics, 2009, first edition in Danish *Mosefolket. Jernalderens mennesker bevaret i 2000 år* (Copenhagen: Glydendal, 1965).

Green, Miranda. "Humans as Ritual Victims in the Later Prehistory of Western Europe." *Oxford Journal of Archaeology* 17, no. 2 (1998): 169–189.

Groen, Linda, and Geert Souwer. "Constructie of reconstructie. Historische gezichten als brug naar het verleden." *Skript. Historisch Tijdschrift* 21, no. 4 (2014): 265–276.

Groen, W., and T. De Ridder. *VLAK verslag 15.3: Gat in de Markt 01.101. Het menselijk botmateriaal uit de periode 1000–1050*, Gemeente Vlaardingen, Stadsarchief en archeologie, August 2007.

Himmler, Heinrich. "Bevölkerungspolitische Rede vor SS-Gruppenführer über die 'Frage der Homosexualität' und ein 'natürliches Verhältnis der Geschlechter zueinander' (1937)." In H. Himmler, *Geheimreden 1933–1945 und andere Ansprachen*, edited by B.F. Smith, 93–104. Propyläen Verlag, Frankfurt am Main, 1974.

Hopkin, Michael. "An Ancient Egyptian Priest Has a Virtual Life at London's British Museum." *Nature* 430 (July 21, 2004).

Joy, Jody. "Looking Death in the Face: Different Attitudes towards Bog Bodies and Their Display with a Focus on Lindow Man." In *Regarding the Dead*, 10–19. London: British Museum Press, 2010.

Kelly, Eamonn P. "Secrets of the Bog Bodies: The Enigma of the Iron Age Explained." *Archaeology Ireland* 20, no. 1 (2006): 26–30; and his "An Archaeological Interpretation of Irish Iron Age Bog Bodies." In *The Archaeology of Violence: Interdisciplinary Approaches*, edited by S. Ralph. New York: State University of New York Press, 2012.

Laqueur, Thomas W. *The Work of the Dead: A Cultural History of Mortal Remains*. Princeton: Princeton University Press, 2015.

Levine, Joshua. "Europe's Famed Bog Bodies Are Starting to Reveal Their Secrets." *Smithsonian Magazine*, May 2017, web-edition.

O'Brian, Barbara. "Do You Remember the Lindow Man Campaign?" *Wilmslow.co.uk*, Tuesday, November 2, 2010. <www.wilmslow.co.uk/news/article/3193/do-you-remember-the-lindow-man-campaign>

Oosterhuis, Harry. "Male Bonding and the Persecution of Homosexual Men in Nazi Germany." *Amsterdams Sociologisch Tijdschrift* 17, no. 4 (1991).

Pilbeam, Pamela. *Madame Tussaud and the History of Waxworks*. London: Hambledon and London, 2003.

Prag, J., and R. Neave. *Making Faces: Using Forensic and Archaeological Evidence*, 168. London: British Museum Press, 1997.

Price, Neil. "The New MOMU: Meeting the Family at Denmark's Flagship Museum of Prehistory and Ethnography." *Antiquity* 89 (2015): 478–484.

Pringle, Heather. *The Master Plan: Himmler's Scholars and the Holocaust*. London, Fourth Estate, 2006.

Ravn, Morten. "Burial in Bogs: Bronze and Early Iron Age Bog Bodies from Denmark." *Acta Archaeologica* 81 (2010): 112–123.

Sanders, Karen. *Bodies in the Bog and the Archaeological Imagination*. Chicago: University of Chicago Press, 2009.

Sitch, Bryan. "Consultation or Confrontation? Lindow Man, a Bog Body Mystery." In *The New Museum Community: Audiences, Challenges, Benefits*, 368–388. Edinburgh: Museumetc, 2010.

Taylor, John H. Daniel Antoine. *Ancient Lives, New Discoveries: Eight Mummies, Eight Stories*. London: The British Museum, 2014.

Van Beek, R., J.H.J. Candel, C. Quick, et al. "The Landscape Setting of Bog Bodies: Interdisciplinary Research into the Site Location of Yde Girl, the Netherlands." *The Holocene* 29, no. 7 (2019): 1206–1222.

Van der Sanden, Wijnand. *Through Nature to Eternity: The Bog Bodies of Northwestern Europe*. Amsterdam: De Bataafsche Leeuw, 1996.

Verhart, Leo. *De reconstructie van Trijntje. Oog in oog met de oudste vrouw van Nederland.* Utrecht, Kosmos Teleac, 2001.

Wilkinson, C.M. "Facial Reconstruction. Anatomical Art or Artistic Anatomy?" *Journal of Anatomy* 216, no. 2 (2010): 235–250.

# 4 Fashion and physique

## Size, shape, and body politics in the display of historical dress

*Emma McClendon*

The twenty-first century has witnessed an explosion of fashion-focused exhibitions at museums around the world. They are some of the most widely publicized and visited events on many museum calendars. Indeed, the exhibition *Heavenly Bodies: Fashion and the Catholic Imagination*, mounted by the Costume Institute at The Metropolitan Museum of Art (The Met), became the most visited exhibition in the museum's history in 2018. Mannequins are a vital component of any fashion exhibition because clothing is inherently linked to the body. To use the words of art and design historian John Potvin, "fashion not only rubs up against our fleshy bodies, but is itself a second skin" (Potvin, 2009, 8). As a cultural practice, clothing is a physical layer that imbues bodies with social meaning. As a museum object, a garment is a three-dimensional, ergonomic, and engineered product of design. When planning a fashion exhibition, a fundamental question thus becomes: "How will the garments be physically displayed?"

There are many factors that affect the answer, including an institution's budget and conservation protocol. The many ways curators and conservators have approached this question expose inherent tensions in the preservation, presentation, and collection of fashion in museums around the world. What takes priority between a designer's "intent" and the way a garment was worn by consumers when a garment is considered for exhibition or dressed on a mannequin? Interest in preserving a designer's intent may lend greater authority to runway shows, advertisements, and magazine editorials as historical records. This could result in an exhibition of small, sample-size garments (or garments pinned to appear smaller) displayed on mannequins that emulate the idealized fashionable physique of models. On the other hand, an interest in how fashion objects were worn in everyday life by consumers and donors may result in a display of a wider variety of body shapes and sizes but will appear different than images seen in historical magazines.

In 2017, I curated an exhibition titled *The Body: Fashion and Physique* at The Museum at The Fashion Institute of Technology (MFIT), which

DOI: 10.4324/9780429260575-4

explored the history of body politics and fashion from the eighteenth century to the present. The process of mounting that show illuminated the tenuous position of the mannequin in the curatorial process, a position that is often overlooked, and given little consideration or analysis. The mannequin is treated as a prop that has been used again and again – an ingredient in the formula of a successful fashion exhibition. However, this outlook belies not only the complex history of the mannequin within the museum as well as the fashion industry, but also its broader social and psychological impact.

Today, the mannequin of fashion exhibitions is typically a tall, thin, white, abstracted homage to the female form, devoid of hair, facial features, and sexual markers (aside from the sinuous curve of small hips and bust). Smooth and white, the fashion mannequin is a stand-in for the feminine ideal. As design historian Emily R. Klug put it, "They are a united breed, the epitome of calculated beauty and meticulous perfection, inspiring the envious glances of women and the admiring stares of men" (Klug, 2009, 200). The museum mannequin is closely linked to the mannequin of retail spaces, particularly store windows, in which "the tall, lithe creatures . . . inspire the consumer and incite the desire to buy" (Klug, 2009, 200). But as Klug points out, this tension between "desire and consumption" is also "inevitably isolating . . . leaving her [the consumer] with feelings of inferiority" (Klug, 2009, 200). The fashion mannequin is a commercial device of marketing. Within the retail space it is clear how its idealized form helps create and project a fantasy, which, in turn, sells product. Such a capitalist agenda is not so clear in the museum gallery, but here the mannequin is still employed to project a fantasy. It is the fantasy of fashion itself. The museum objects are not just clothes within the gallery space, they are fashion. The mannequin helps imbue the display with gravitas and credibility. How are visitors supposed to appreciate the importance of the fashion objects on view if they do not resemble what we are used to seeing, consuming, and understanding as fashionable?

Sarah Scaturro, head conservator at The Met's Costume Institute, spoke of this when discussing the role of the conservator in fashion exhibitions: "For fashion conservation to be successful, objects must be rendered as just that – fashion" (Scatturo, 2018, 33). According to Scaturro, a conservator's approach exists on a spectrum and "some fashion conservation treatments might align more closely to restoration owing to the aestheticized mandate to present the objects as *fashion*"[1] (Scatturo, 2018, 33). She acknowledges the "sticky problem of artistic intent, a nebulous concept that privileges the maker's design as the *ne plus ultra*" (Scatturo, 2018, 33). But in fashion, intent equals the runways and editorials that project the fantasy of the designer's creative vision, not the reality of what a garment looked like on the street when worn by the women who purchase the fantasy. Within the fantasy of fashion, the female body is malleable, something that can be molded and changed with the cut of a garment, sculpting underwear, diet, exercise, and even plastic surgery. Today, the fashion body is forever-young, tall, thin, and almost always white. This ideal exists in the museum in the form of the mannequin.

It is worth noting that the debate over the importance of designer intent versus consumer practice also includes, at its crux, the mission of the institution mounting a particular exhibition. Fashion exhibitions appear in museums across disciplines – at those dedicated to fine art, social history, and fashion, among others. Each type of museum might have a tendency to prioritize one view of fashion over another. The art museum might skew towards the designer as artist/creator, while the social history museum might wish to emphasize the person who wore and donated a particular ensemble. But it can also be the opposite, depending on an exhibition's theme: an art museum might want to highlight the collection or wardrobe of a noted client; likewise, the social history museum might wish to show a collective fashionable aesthetic that defined a socio-cultural movement. Whatever the goal of the institution, fashion exhibitions engage in body politics through mannequin choice, and this engagement carries meaning beyond the theme of a show or the walls of a museum.

The prototypical lithe, white fashion mannequin reaffirms certain body types while marginalizing others. To view the mannequin as mere prop within a museum is to deny the potent power of a dressed body. By placing the fashion mannequin prominently within the museum space, fashion exhibitions contribute to the construction of body image ideals by suggesting what types of bodies deserve to be visible and remembered.

## The "ideal"

In 1985, fashion historian Elizabeth Wilson famously declared, "There is something eerie about a museum of costume" (Wilson, 1985, 1). For her, "The deserted gallery seems haunted. The living observer moves, with a sense of mounting panic, through a world of the dead . . . when we gaze at garments that had an intimate relationship with human beings long since gone to their graves" (Wilson, 1985, 1). This view of the fashion museum as a "tableau mort" (to borrow Denise Witzig's term) has pervaded much of the scholarship on fashion exhibitions and curatorial practice (Witzig in Petrov, 2019, 138). While I may not ascribe to this view myself, it provides a useful starting point to consider the history of the fashion mannequin. It seems logical that an intense desire to reject the deathliness inherent in the display of dead people's clothing lies at the root of the trend towards ever-increasing theatricality and glamour in today's most popular fashion exhibitions. These fantastical exhibitions employ the visual vocabulary of the retail environment and fashion media to infuse museum displays with "life."

There has always been a connection between the display of fashion in retail spaces and museums, particularly at the most basic level of raw materials such as mannequins. Historian and curator Julia Petrov's book *Fashion, History, Museums* offers a thorough account of the evolution of historical dress in museums in the United States and Europe. She cites a 1911 display of historical fashion by the Museum of London at Kensington Palace as the "first instance of a major public museum in the English-speaking world putting on a display of historical fashion" (Petrov, 2019, 2, 15). But she notes that contemporary reviewers did not see anything "startlingly novel" in the display, suggesting that viewers were accustomed to the look of dressed forms, or proxy-bodies, from earlier forms of displays (Petrov, 2019, 31–61). One key example Petrov cites is the displays by waxwork museums, such as Madame Tussauds, which created likenesses of famous historical figures in wax with uncanny verisimilitude.

Petrov also cites the importance of window shopping (Petrov, 2019, 31–61). During the late-nineteenth century, electric lighting, advancements in glass production, and mass-manufactured, lifelike mannequins came together to create a new form of spectacle and amusement for city dwellers – it was window shopping as leisure activity. Department store mannequins were often also made of wax in the late nineteenth century in both Europe and the United States. Osborne notes that Gem Wax Models began distributing wax mannequins to U.S. department stores in 1885 (Osborne, 2019, 187), but these mannequins were not crafted to recreate a particular person's likeness in the style of the wax museum. Instead, they were idealized to sell a fantasy. Here is the divide between the morbidity of the historical wax effigy and the vitality of the theatrical shop window mannequin. The 1911 exhibition at Kensington Palace used wooden forms "without hands or feet" to dress the objects, suggesting a discomfort on the part of the museum staff at aligning their display with either the wax museum or the department store. When the *First Ladies Collection* opened at the Smithsonian in 1916, the museum took a different approach and specially commissioned white mannequins. The mannequins had facial features and hair rendered in plaster, but rather than emulating the visage of the First Ladies themselves, the features were idealized and slightly abstracted to recall neo-classical sculpture. A goal of these sculptural mannequins was likely to draw attention to the garments, rather than "uncanny persons" (Petrov, 2019, 160), that is, Smithsonian visitors were meant to examine the dresses, not what they were dressed on. Nevertheless, the idealized look of the smooth, white figures, positioned the "First Lady" as an archetype of American femininity. This strategy avoided Wilson's morbidity of staring at the dresses of dead women on literal effigies of the deceased. But by negating each First Lady's individuality (as well as her true likeness) the white plaster mannequins made the gallery into a fantasy – a fantasy that suggested (however unintentionally) the faces and physiques of the actual First Ladies were not "fashion" worthy.

Today the Smithsonian uses headless, invisible forms to display the First Lady dresses. "Invisible" forms are mounts that are custom-made to the dimensions of a garment and designed to support the garment internally without extending beyond its boundaries –that is, they have no heads, hands, or feet that might be visible past a hemline, sleeve, or collar. They can be constructed from a combination of buckram, ethafoam, wood, lightweight plexi, and the more recently developed material Fosshape.[2] Thus, the Smithsonian display manages to show each First Lady's actual size and shape without rendering an eerie effigy. However, most institutions still consider abstracted sinewy mannequins the default way to display fashion as both a dynamic, living practice while also keeping the focus on the garments. As English curator Doris Langley Moore would describe in the 1960s,

> After experimenting over many years with display techniques, I have found that dummies which look human, with just the degree of idealization that has always been a feature of successful fashion plates, serve our purpose much better than headless and armless or highly stylized models. . . . Realism certainly ought not to be as obtrusive as in waxwork portraiture, but those to whom costume is an unfamiliar subject will find little interest in a sleeve with deep ruffles unless it is set off by an arm.
>
> (Petrov, 2019, 160)

Moore founded what is now known as the Fashion Museum in Bath in 1963. During her tenure with the collection, she indeed experimented with a wide variety of display methods including a rather ingenious method of mounting historical garments on enlarged, life-size reproductions of period illustrations and paintings (Petrov, 2019, 153). This placed three-dimensional clothing within the two-dimensional ground of the mural. However, the illustrations still presented an idealized view of the past with their stylized, drawn bodies that abstracted the fleshy reality of the men and women who would have actually worn the garments. This approach also served to align fashion with methods of fine art display by literally placing the garments in a mural. Given this proclivity towards idealization, it comes as little surprise that Moore would favor an approach of "mannequins as sculptures" (as Petrov put it) when using three-dimensional forms (Petrov, 2019, 160).

Today, the most common and recognizable fashion mannequin is the schläppi (Figure 4.1). To quote the Bonaveri website (the Italian company that manufactures schläppi mannequins), "The Schläppi Collections represent some of the world's most enduring forms, used by fashion houses since the 1960s" (Bonaveri, 2019). These mannequins venture decidedly further into abstraction from Moore's "dummies which look human, with just the degree of idealization" (Petrov, 2019, 160). The schläppi lies somewhere on the spectrum between fashion model and alien with their bald, shiny heads, impossibly long necks, legs, and arms, punctuated by sinuous fingers and merely the subtlest of indentations and protrusions to suggest eyes, nose, and mouth. Perhaps the schläppi is best understood as the three-dimensional manifestation of a croquis – a figure outline commonly drawn by fashion students. The croquis is the form on which garments can be sketched and drafted on paper. In other words, it is the industry standard ideal.

As the Bonaveri website suggests, schläppis are not just used in museums. They appear in retail spaces around the world – department stores, boutiques, etc. Here again is the link between the shop and the museum. Not only is the schläppi idealized, it codes the museum gallery as a "fashion" space. You are looking at "fashion" – not clothes – as evidenced by the high fashion forms. The schläppi is a stylized statue, not an effigy. The schläppi is glamour, not morbid. The only difference between the schläppi in the store window, and the one in the museum, is that the museum mannequin is outfitted with a protective layer underneath the garments to separate the objects from the mannequin itself.

Unlike other types of mannequins, a schläppi's head is not removable, but the arms, legs, and hands are. This makes it easier to dress garments on an inanimate form, but it also gives curators and retail designers different pose options. An institution can commission special custom versions if the budget allows. In the museum, the pose of a mannequin is based on the capabilities of the garments as well as the mannequin's planned position within the gallery space. Each pose is unquestionably "fashionable" as if pulled from the editorial pages of *Vogue*. Like the schläppi's smooth proportions, the position of its limbs transforms the exhibition platform into a fashion tableau.

I have used schläppis in many past exhibitions. Because they are the most common fashion mannequin, museums that have regular fashion exhibitions often have them in stock supply. In 2015, I co-curated the exhibition *Yves Saint Laurent + Halston: Fashioning the 70s* with The Museum at FIT (MFIT) deputy director Patricia Mears. For that show we consciously used only white schläppis, for a couple of reasons. One, we were only looking at garments produced from roughly 1965–1985, so we did not have to worry about dressing any historical silhouettes. A common issue with mannequin

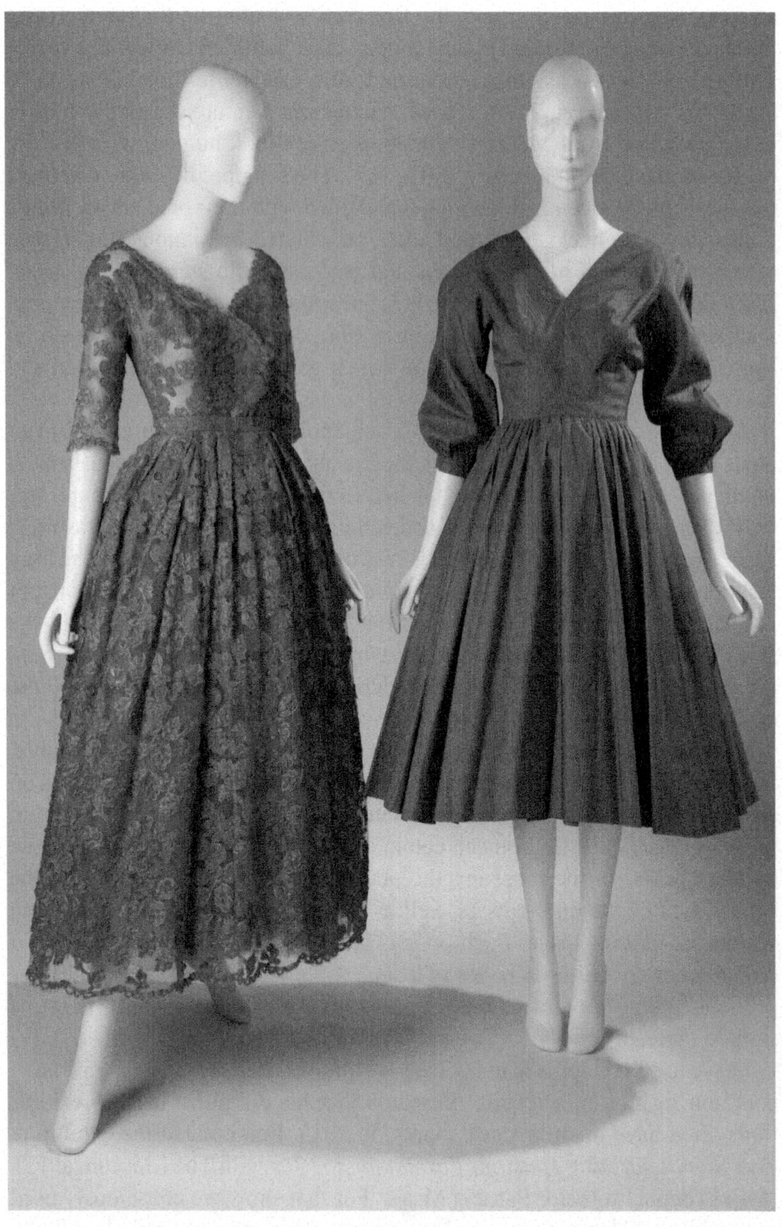

*Figure 4.1* Schläppi mannequins dressed in Dior (left) and Anne Fogarty (right) from The Museum at FIT collection.

*Source:* Image courtesy of The Museum at FIT.

choice in fashion exhibitions is that, unlike a fleshy body, a rigid mannequin cannot adjust to the shape of historical garments (i.e. corsets) that were designed to mold the body. For such pieces, special mannequins are typically used, which have been cast in a corseted shape. If an institution can afford it, historical garments can be dressed on contemporary fashion mannequins, but it requires invasive work on the mannequin that will likely render it unusable in the future. Mannequins will be cut into, sawed apart, and reassembled to create a shape for a garment to close around.

Another reason for using all-white schläppis was that we created an all-white set for the show. The platforms, walls, and floor were all rendered in a high-gloss white in order to evoke the modern minimalism of the 1970s era and highlight the saturated colors both men often worked with in their designs. The goal of the show was to offer a close reading of the design techniques and methodologies employed by two of the most famous fashion designers of the twentieth century when they were each at the peak of their careers. The uniform fleet of all-white schläppis was intended to blend into the larger set and underscore the garments as the focus.

Here, the mannequins were props, a design feature of the gallery. We did not consider them part of the content of the exhibition itself. By 2015, the schläppi form had become so recognizable, common, and expected within the space of the fashion exhibition, that it seemed as if it could fade into the background. When I began work on *The Body: Fashion and Physique* a little over a year later I found myself confronted with the inescapable presence of the schläppi and began to come to terms with the profound and problematic impact it has. And while I will be chiefly discussing the issue of size here, it is important to acknowledge that the (tall, thin, *white*) fashion mannequin is problematic on many levels, not least of which is its negation of race. As Petrov has put it:

> Featured or featureless, mannequins are most often painted a "neutral" white . . . and have Caucasian features . . . thus erasing any ethnic diversity that may have been present in the individuals who originally wore the clothes. . . .While it can be argued that much of the fashion objects held in museums are elite examples, and historically, the elite classes of the Western world have been overwhelmingly Caucasian, to literally whitewash out the embodied markers of race in order to fit a visual priority is an example of the privileged nature of aesthetics in museum discourse.
>
> (Petrov, 2019, 165)

In 2011, The Met unveiled its groundbreaking exhibition *Alexander McQueen: Savage Beauty*. The show shocked the world with astounding visitor numbers and thrust fashion exhibitions into the spotlight. The exhibition itself was mounted on sinewy, schläppi-esque mannequins in mainly white, but also silver; their blank faces obscured by masks of fabric. Within the catalogue, each garment appeared on a similarly white, lithe mannequin, but here the mannequins were twisted and contorted into incredibly dynamic and lifelike poses – completely unlike any mannequins seen before. This was achieved by actually foregoing the traditional mannequin completely, and using a live human model instead, here painted white and then digitally manipulated to look like a mannequin in the finished images. During the photography shoot the models had strings tied around their wrists, necks, and torsos to mimic the joints where a mannequin's arms, hands, legs, and head can be removed and reassembled. These lines were then further enhanced in digital post-production. At this stage, the models' heads were either digitally edited out or replaced with the blank, bald head of the fashion mannequin to complete the transformation (Wilson, 2011).

The Met was able to take this approach because almost all of the works in the exhibition were loans from the Alexander McQueen company archive – meaning they were not museum objects. Today, museums prohibit collection objects from being dressed and photographed on live models, but as property of a fashion house, these garments could be treated as live fashion the way a garment on an editorial shoot might be. But why go to such extremes to make models into mannequins if you can use live models? As we have seen, the "deathliness" of the mannequin (and how to overcome it) has been at the core of fashion curatorial practice for over a century. To make model into mannequin is a testament to the symbolic power of the mannequin within the museum in the twenty-first century.

According to a *New York Times* article, curator Andrew Bolton felt that "to make models look like mannequins . . . spoke to the blurring of boundaries . . . that was a consistent theme of the McQueen collections" (Wilson, 2011). However, the article noted that the decision was also vital because, "It was important that its [the catalog's] imagery convey the authority of the museum, not a fashion magazine" (Wilson, 2011). In 2011, the white, lithe mannequin had become a symbol of authority – intellectual, cultural, and fashionable. The Met wanted lifelike, fashion poses in the extreme, but to completely abandon the mannequin would have aligned the catalog too closely with the visual language of the editorial, and commercialism by extension. The desired result was images that "look as if they had been composed in the traditional academic style of previous exhibition catalogs" but which also went beyond the confines of that medium (Wilson, 2011). In other words, these images are a fantasy. A fantasy of a mannequin that is neither dead nor fully alive. A female body in full service of curatorial vision, immediately recognizable as both fashionable and academically serious. This is the true ideal embodied by the fashion mannequin.

## The "real"

When I began planning *The Body: Fashion and Physique* in 2016, mannequins were a central concern from the show's inception. The exhibition looked at the ideal fashionable physique as a cultural construct, one that has shifted throughout history to emphasize different shapes and proportions. We can see this is the construction of garments, in the strategies designers use to draw the eye – for example, by changing the placement of a waistline, the fullness of a sleeve, the volume of a skirt. So, in part, the exhibition dealt with a history of silhouette; but it went beyond silhouette to consider body politics, how bodies have been portrayed and treated by the fashion industry, how certain bodies have been celebrated but how others have been marginalized and stigmatized. Because the fashion industry operates around an idealized fantasy body that it projects through marketing, I wanted to grapple with what the "real" lived experience was for people consuming and wearing fashion. To do this, I knew we had to convey the diversity of shapes and sizes represented by garments within the MFIT collection across historical periods. The uniform and idealized proportions of the schläppi were antithetical to this goal. I did not want garments draped over abstracted versions of white models – their sinewy necks and mannerist hands protruding from the edges of each garment. However, I had to work within the material and budgetary boundaries of the project as well.

*The Body* was mounted in MFIT's Fashion and Textile History Gallery. This space is dedicated to displaying the museum's permanent collection. Unlike a museum of fine art that might leave the same paintings and sculptures from its permanent collection on display for decades at a time, clothing is much too fragile to continuously display. In order to ensure the longevity of the pieces in its collection, MFIT redisplays its permanent galleries every six months. This "rotation" is viewed as an opportunity to explore the history of fashion through a new theme, and to display objects that have never been on view before as well as acquire new pieces to fill gaps in the collection. To meet these needs, History Gallery exhibitions cannot have loans, they need to be able to be installed quickly and efficiently to ensure the permanent galleries are not "dark" (i.e. closed) for more than two weeks, and they need to adhere to a strict (tight) budget. Budget is always a key factor in mannequin choice for an exhibition. Mannequins cost upwards of $1500 USD each. To buy even one can drastically cut into a tight exhibition budget, much less purchasing an entire set of new mannequins to make a "uniform" display. On a tight budget, a curator needs to figure out how to work with the materials available.

I chose to display each object on a dress form. Logistically, MFIT has a large stock of dress forms from different periods, so it would not be a budgetary issue to use them. However, the dress form was appropriate from a thematic perspective as well. The dress form is a tool used in the draping and fitting of a garment as it is made. It seemed appropriate conceptually to include dress forms throughout the exhibition since they are intimately involved in the process of bringing garments from idea to finished product. They are the proxy-bodies within the space of the designer studio. In fact, I chose to begin the exhibition with a display of historical dress forms from the nineteenth and twentieth centuries in order to demonstrate how the shape of the mannequins used within the fashion industry itself have changed. They too are a cultural construct that has shifted drastically over time. As the website for leading dress form manufacturer Wolf Form explains, since its founding in the 1990s, "the female shape has changed and evolved as each new 'look' came into fashion. Wolf Forms have constantly kept pace with these fashion trends, interpreting and incorporating them into every Wolf Form" (Wolf Form).

We used mainly Wolf Forms in the exhibition in tandem with other types of dress forms and custom forms. On an aesthetic level, the dress forms allowed the garments to appear as if they were floating above the platform. Conservator Marjorie Jonas built out a custom form to fit one of the garments for *The Body* (Figure 4.2). The images show how, starting from a standard Wolf Form, she slowly built up the shape of the form to the measurements of the dress

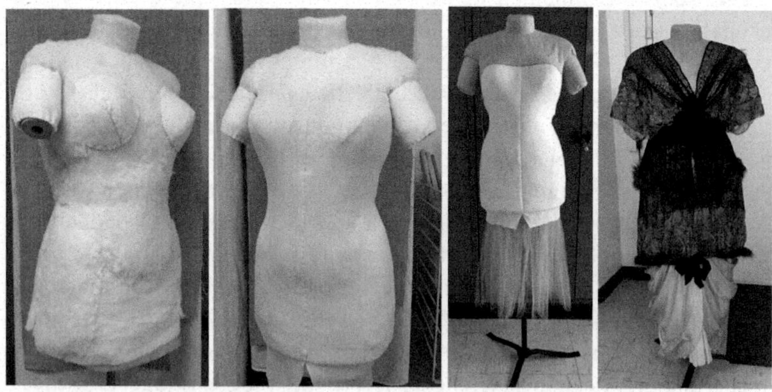

*Figure 4.2* Installation view of *The Body: Fashion and Physique*, 2017.

*Source:* Image courtesy of The Museum at FIT.

using a combination of poly felt and polyester batting. Once she achieved the desired dimensions, she covered the torso with an off-white stockinette, and then covered the neck and chest with a slightly darker raw silk to mimic the look of the original Wolf Form. Without heads, arms, or legs, dress forms gave shape to the garments without imposing a "stylized" body beyond their boundaries. There was no mannequin pose or idealized proportion, just the garment in its full measurements as it would have been worn.

Of course, the floating or "invisible" approach does have its challenges. Petrov cites the 2008 exhibition *Reveal or Conceal?* at the McCord Museum in Montreal as an example, specifically a section devoted to the social importance of the changing length of skirts (i.e. the changing amount of leg exposed). In Petrov's words, "High hemlines expose the female leg, but in an exhibition where mannequins are not possessed of limbs, all that is exposed are awkwardly empty shoes, placed under an improbably floating dress" (Petrov, 2019, 158). This issue is both logistical and narrative. It is difficult to display certain objects on dress forms and floating mounts because most forms do not have legs. For *The Body* we did locate a few with legs, but they were hanged from an industrial-looking stand and did appear quite "haunted" (to use Wilson's word). Ultimately, I felt this "eeriness" served the narrative goal of the exhibition: the relationship between the fashion industry and the consumer body is not a nice one – it is disturbing. However, I admit that such forms are not appropriate within the display of every show. If an institution has a sizeable budget, special mannequins could be purchased or commissioned. In fact, many major institutions do purchase all (or many) new mannequins for "blockbuster" exhibitions. It makes one wonder why we continue to see the same waif mannequins again and again in these highly publicized events? Again, here is the tension between the "ideal" and the "real," between the fantasy of a designer's intent versus female consumers. Which deserves to be represented in the museum? I argue that the two should not be treated as mutually exclusive. It should be possible to represent the designer's fullest intent at any size.

The "invisible" approach is not new. Museums have experimented with padded and invisible mounts in varying forms since the earliest displays of historical dress. Indeed, as already mentioned, when the first permanent exhibition of historical dress opened at Kensington Palace in 1911 it was mounted on forms that did not have hands or feet. When the Victoria and Albert Museum redesigned its fashion galleries in 1983, the new display used invisible mounts without heads, hands, or feet. Sir Roy Strong, the museum director at that time, applauded the new approach saying,

> Dress is the sculpture of fabric on the human body. It has an aesthetic form. We are not trying to present it as part of an illustrate book or as

> the social history of Jane Austen's world. . . . This display is anti-camp, anti-dramatic, anti-theatre . . . the real innovation of this exhibition [was the] human element. Each of the 200 figures has been exactly proportioned to fit the garments of display, instead of pinning and folding the clothes to the dummies.
>
> (Petrov, 2019, 151)

This process of "pinning and folding the clothes to the dummies" that Strong mentions is one of the least discussed practices in mounting fashion exhibitions. Institutions, curators, and conservators have different attitudes towards it throughout the field, and there are also varying techniques applied. However, what the practice ultimately involves is manipulating a garment in some manner to *appear* as if it fits the mannequin being used, and this manipulation is almost always to make the garment appear smaller (although it can also be done to make a garment fit a form that is too big for it – for instance, a garment may not be fully closed at the back and then this is obscured by the position of the mannequin on a platform).

This practice literally distorts the historical object and our understanding of history with it. There is a common misconception that all women of the past were smaller than we are today, and were the same size. Some believe that women of the nineteenth century, for instance, all had eighteen-inch waists. Objects show that this is not the case – *if* you allow them to be displayed in their true dimensions. In *The Body*, I included two corsets from the 1880s side-by-side (Figure 4.3). The black measured approximately 20 inches around the waist, while the pink one measured 32 inches. We dressed the black one slightly open at the back to demonstrate the variability in how women would wear their corsets. They were not always "tight-laced." In fact, so-called "tight-lacing" was actually quite rare, despite our popular perception of corsets today (Steele, 2001). It was common to vary the tightness of a corset depending on the occasion, in some instances leaving as much as an inch open in the back. In a case beneath the corsets was a mail-order catalogue from the same period. Below each corset style, the catalog listed the measurements available, several in 18–36 inches. The length of an inch has not changed. The anatomy of the body has not changed. It is our contemporary culture and biases that have shaped our understanding of history. When a garment is pinned, or folded, or discreetly padded to make a garment *look* smaller than it is, the museum alters history. Visitors do not know they are looking at stagecraft. It is deceit in the service of curatorial aesthetics.

I have previously written on this practice in relation to the work of historian Michel-Rolph Trouillot (McClendon, 2019). For Trouillot, "history begins with bodies and artifacts" (Trouillot, 1995, 29). Museum exhibitions

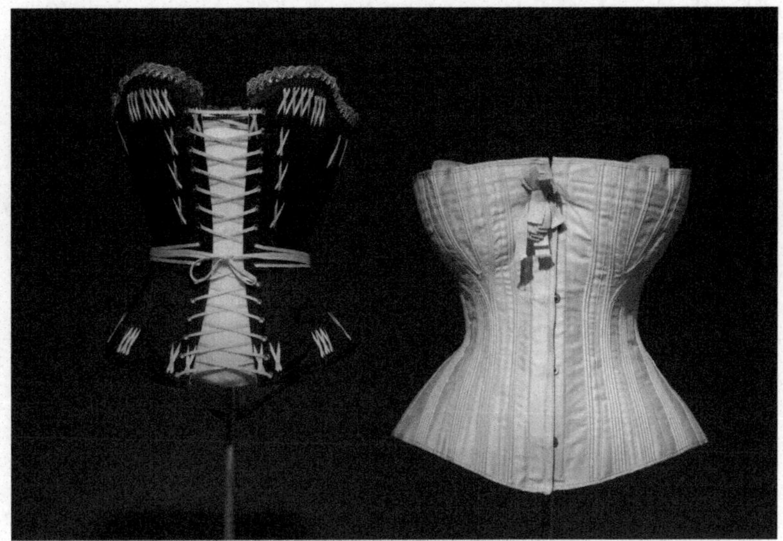

*Figure 4.3* Installation view of *The Body: Fashion and Physique*, 2017.

*Source:* Image courtesy of The Museum at FIT.

and archives are keepers of historical records, but as he explains, they too are subject to power dynamics. They are built, conceived of, and created by people – people with their own biases, political views, and motivations that inform on their work, however subtly. In his words, "Historical representations – be they books, commercial exhibits or public commemorations – cannot be conceived only as vehicles for the transmission of knowledge. They must establish some relation to that knowledge" (Trouillot, 1995, 149). And in that relationship between historical sources and their producers we find "silences" – pockets of neglect and negation. For Trouillot, "any historical narrative is a particular bundle of silences" (Trouillot, 1995, 27). Historical silence is the result of a power imbalance. In museums we see this in the "uneven power in the production of sources, archives, and narratives" (Trouillot, 1995, 27). Pinning, padding, and manipulating a historical garment creates a silence. The corporeal reality of the person who wore it is excised from its display.

Not all objects are pinned and padded in exhibitions. In fact, in a typical exhibition, the number of manipulated pieces will be a small minority. Smaller sizes tend to populate the fashion collections of the world, but this should not be taken as evidence of women's body sizes through history. As Trouillot has taught us, collections are built by people, people with their own biases. Fashion collections are often misinterpreted as records of female physiology. Petrov quotes a *New York Times* article from 1911, which discusses a recent acquisition by The Met of a collection of historical garments from the Ludlow family. The quote reads:

> The costumes present an interesting subject for those interested in the development of the American woman. The average girl today could not begin to get into the gowns of the girl of the early part of the nineteenth century or into those of her mother fifty years before. . . . The dresses show that the women of that time were short as well as small, and the Museum authorizes had infinite trouble finding manikins [sic] over which to gowns could be fitted to show them properly. Figures are not made that size now, as there are only the exceptional women so small.
> (Petrov, 2019, 146–147)

As Petrov astutely points out, "It does not seem to have occurred to the author of the piece that the Ludlow women could themselves have been exceptional" (Petrov, 2019, 147). An unfortunate fact of fashion collections is that smaller sizes are favored for acquisition. Lauren Downing Peters has dubbed this phenomenon "survival bias" (Neilson, 2017). The preference for smaller-sized garments is often justified as a way to ensure that the objects in a collection will best represent the designer intent as seen in the historical record of magazines and runways – records that negate the "real" consumer in favor of models. The preference for smaller sizes is also justified as a way to ensure a garment can be "used" – that is, be dressed for exhibition on "standard" mannequins. Here again is the power of the mannequin. Because mannequins have become such a critical element of an exhibition display, they affect what is preserved. Rather than viewing the mannequin as a tool that can be manipulated and put to the service of an exhibition, budgetary restrictions and aesthetic expectations have placed mannequin over object. The clothes (and collection) are fit to the mannequins when it should be the other way around.

It is worth noting that Peters is an expert in the history of plus-size fashion. Aside from the power dynamics and biases at play in the acquisition process, she also identifies another blind spot in "survival bias." While plus-size fashion was an important component of *The Body* (at MFIT we are lucky enough to have examples of early, ready-to-wear, plus-size clothing), Peters has noted that a criterion for objects collected by museums is that often they were made by "noteworthy" designers (Neilson, 2017). In an industry that systemically marginalizes and ignores the production of "plus-size" garments, how can a plus-size designer ever be considered noteworthy? As a result, plus-size fashion has been silenced in the record of fashion history.

Thus the "real" body is as murky as the "ideal" one within the museum. Even a show like *The Body* that strives to show a diversity of body shapes and sizes is limited by what has survived. But creating forms that display the full proportions of every garment, no matter its shape or size, at least begins to give a sense of the individuality that has always existed in the wearing of fashion.

## Conclusion

We cannot deny that biases and body politics have played a role in how fashion has been displayed within the space of the museum over the last century. The mannequin has been at the center of this history. It is a standard prop that carries both fashionable and academic gravitas. But the mannequin is a tool. It is a technology. As we move further into the twenty-first century we should think beyond the "standard" that has been set, to how we can begin to shine light into the dark spaces of historical silence.

I interviewed Model Alliance founder Sara Ziff for a video that played in the first room of *The Body*. The Model Alliance is a non-profit labor advocacy organization with a mission of promoting "fair treatment, equal opportunity, and sustainable practices in the fashion industry, from the runway to the factory floor" (Model Alliance). When speaking about the runway and its continued lack of diversity she put into words what so many have been feeling recently: "It can't at this point just be about the clothes, it also has to be about who's wearing them." This principle applies to the museum space as well. At this point, an exhibition cannot just be about the clothes, it has to also be about what they are shown on.

## Notes

1 Italics appear in original source.

2 For more detailed information on the construction methods employed in invisible mounts please see Cynthia Amneus' and Marla Miles' article "A Method for Invisibly Mounting Costume Using Fosshape," *Journal of the American Institute for Conservation* 51, no. 1 (2012): 3–14. It is important to acknowledge that I am not a conservator. Conservators are the individuals trained to actually dress, mount, and install historical dress objects. They require a complex technical training and expertise. My rudimentary explanation of different mounts here does not do their work justice.

## References

Bonaveri Company Website. Accessed July 11, 2019. <https://bonaveri.com/collections/schlappi/>

Klug, Emily R. "Allure of the Silent Beauties: Mannequins and Display in America, 1935–70." In *The Places and Spaces of Fashion, 1800–2007*, edited by John Potvin. New York: Routledge, 2009.

McClendon, Emma. "The Body: Fashion and Physique: A Curatorial Discussion." In *Fashion Theory*, Volume 23, 147–165. London: Taylor & Francis, 2019.

Model Alliance Mission Statement. Accessed October 4, 2019. <https://modelalliance.org/mission>

Neilson, Laura. "How Museums and Cultural Institutions Have Shaped the History of Body Diversity." on website *Fashionista*, December 6, 2017, Accessed July 5, 2018. <https://fashionista.com/2017/12/mannequins-fashion-museum-fit-body-exhibit>

Osborne, Vanessa. "The Logic of the Mannequin: Shop Windows and the Realist Novel." In Potvin, 2019, 186.

Petrov, Julia. *Fashion, History, Museums: Inventing the Display of Dress*. New York: Bloomsbury, 2019.

Potvin, John. *The Places and Spaces of Fashion, 1800–2007*, 8. New York: Routledge, 2009.

Scaturro, Sarah. "Confronting Fashion's Death Drive: Conservation, Ghost Labor, and the Material Turn with Fashion Curation." In *Fashion Curating: Critical Practice in the Museum and Beyond*, 33. London: Bloomsbury, 2018.

Steele, Valerie. *The Corset: A Cultural History*, 87–111. New Haven and London: Yale University Press, 2001.

Trouillot, Michel-Roth. *Silencing the Past: Power and the Production of History*, 29. Boston: Beacon Press, 1995.

Wilson, Elizabeth. *Adorned in Dreams: Fashion and Modernity*, 1Ibid. Berkeley, CA: University of California Press, 1985.

Wilson, Eric. "A Mannequin in Every Sense." *The New York Times*, April 13, 2011. Accessed July 11, 2019. <www.nytimes.com/2011/04/14/fashion/14ROW.html>

Wolf Form Company Description on Official Website. Accessed October 4, 2019. <www.wolfforms.com/about-us/>

# 5 Asian physiques of mannequins in American art museums

*Kyunghee Pyun*

In this chapter, I discuss how mannequins were ordered for customized needs and used for various art museum exhibitions to display Asian bodies. I want to draw attention to a bigger issue encompassing both the high-brow culture of art museum visitors and the low-brow consumption of Asian bodies in the context of visual and material culture. Hjemdahl and Steele, fashion historians and curators, have noted that "the distinction between absence and presence of body is not clear-cut and needs to be nuanced and explored" (2014) (Steele, 1998). This view is not only important for dress exhibitions in art museums – which have become more and more popular in the recent decades – but it is also relevant to archaeological objects and fine art works of painting, sculpture, furniture, metalwork, and decorative arts in which bodies and body parts could be viewed in different configurations within the contexts of time, geography, race, and ethnicity.

## From the exotic to the visible: mannequins in the age of world's fairs and expositions

In the nineteenth century, imperial nations hosted world's fairs and expositions, and subsequently established anthropology museums to educate about different human races and their lifestyles (Sandberg, 2003). In the spirit of world's fairs, these museums in Europe presented members of Indigenous tribes from remote places, while some entrepreneurs organized public displays in the form of performance for paid audiences. Sadiah Qureshi, social historian of race, convincingly argues that this type of human exhibition was commercially profitable in spite of its harsh impact on performers' lives (2011). The origin of exhibition dummies and realistic mannequins in museums is traced back to the tradition of human exhibition. Stereotypes of Asian physique had already been created and circulated at these shows in conjunction with or perhaps inspired by pictorial representations of Asian peoples. Historiography of anthropological museums confirms Qureshi's conclusion that the exhibitions

DOI: 10.4324/9780429260575-5

of human races left a lasting legacy both in the formation of anthropology as a discipline and in the creation of public misconceptions of racial differences. Before the development of live human beings as models is perused, we need to think about the invention of the word, mannequins (Greczy, 2018).

It was the late nineteenth century when Charles Frederick Worth (1825–1895), a British couturier who founded the House of Worth in Paris, started using mannequins, which then meant live human beings – mostly anonymous young women – who dressed themselves in fancy clothing designed by Worth and posed for his clients. These women were not professional models but rather worked within the studio as seamstresses or sales assistants (Cumming, Cunnington, and Cunnington, 2010). Lucy Duff-Gordon (1863–1935), the English designer known as Lucile, coined the name *mannequin* for these live models, and Paul Poiret (1879–1944) creatively put them to use in his marketing prints. Much later, in the 1970s, the term was almost obsolete in English, replaced by the word *model*. Birth of the word mannequin in the nineteenth century does not have any connotation for people of other races or ethnicities. Live clothing models for these fashion boutiques were almost always "representative" of desirable body types of wealthy consumers.

## From the visible to the invisible: Asian dolls and absence of mannequins for Asian clothing and textiles in art exhibitions

Mannequins with wigs and facial details became less frequently utilized in both Western and non-Western art exhibitions beginning in the 1960s.[1] At encyclopedic museums such as the Metropolitan Museum of Art or the Brooklyn Museum, for example, mannequins for the Asian armor were faceless. These faceless mannequins for Asian warriors are in stark contrast with mannequins in Asian historical museums where the "brave" generals or the "heroic" soldiers are often portrayed in realistic expressions on the face, with the facial details such as beards or eyebrows painted or glued.[2]

Aware of this legacy coming from natural history museums and the fields of ethnography and anthropology, curators of art museums were careful to stay away from "life groups" dioramas. They focused on Asian fine art such as painting, calligraphy, Buddhist sculpture, and ceramics in a purely aesthetic context of European fine arts as opposed to crafts, historical objects, or material culture. Pioneers of Asian art history such as Benjamin Rowland, Jr. (1904–1972), Alexander Soper (1904–1993), Laurence Sickman (1907–1988), Sherman E. Lee (1918–2008), and John M. Rosenfield (1924–2013) have influenced a generation of curators of Asian art and cultivated an image of intellectual and sophisticated connoisseurs of Asian painting, calligraphy, and religious sculpture, well-versed with classical literature or religious scriptures. This concentration on authenticity, connoisseurship, and development of artistic styles in curatorial activities did not facilitate use of mannequins for Asian clothing and textiles exhibitions. Another important trend in visual representation of Asian clothing and objects was the adaptation of these artifacts, whether historical or contemporary, by cultural cross-dressers in the West. For cultural cross-dressing involving Asian physique, there could be two cases: Asians dress themselves in non-Asian garments, and Westerners dress themselves in Asian dresses. For those living in North America, the latter is abundantly found in fine arts and mass media. In American film and theater, this cross-dressing act is often called the "Yellow Face," a practice of non-Asian actors playing roles of Asian characters.

This fashionable adaptation of Asian clothing by Westerners was already popular in nineteenth century painting during the *Japonisme* movement. Known as an enthusiastic reception of Japanese art and design by the French artists in the mid-nineteenth century, *Japonisme* swept not only France but also other European countries, as manifested in works by artists of Impressionism, Post-Impressionism, and Art Nouveau until the early twentieth century. An example of cultural cross dressing would be found in *Harmony in Blue and Gold: The Peacock Room*, created by James McNeill Whistler in 1876–1877. The Peacock Room contains a centerpiece painting known as *La Princesse du pays de la porcelain* or *Rose and Silver: The Princess from the Land of Porcelain* that Whistler had painted a decade earlier in 1865. The woman in Kimono is not Japanese, but a Greek immigrant in Britain whom Whistler asked to pose for this painting. This type of cultural cross-dressing was so ubiquitous that many do not notice the exotic nature of the painting. Another painting of a European lady – Claude Monet's *La Japonaise* – shows the model, Camille Monet, in a Japanese kimono and a blonde wig, emphasizing her Western features. Ethnographic self-fashioning is a process which involves "increased self-consciousness about the fashioning of human identity as a manipulatable, artful process" (Greenblatt, 1980). In this process, an individual assumes the authority to control and purposely determine his/her own identity. This involves the linking of "cultural artifacts" drawn from discrepant worlds in ways that reflect the individual's own subjective experience (Clifford, 2002). There are numerous well-known examples of such self-conscious bridging of cultures, especially in anthropology (e.g. Bronisław Malinowski) and in literature (e.g. Joseph Conrad) (Gould and Stinerock, 1992).

In this context, curators in art museums wanted to stay away from "life groups" and to disassociate themselves with Orientalism. More and more, they focused on the scientific analysis and the aesthetic quality of Asian art.[3] To display clothing and textiles, curators used garment hangers instead of mannequins as if to emphasize the flatness of the garment construction.[4] The changing silhouettes of historical garments, from both Asian and non-Asian heritage collections, requires adaptable body types that accommodate fashionable bodies (Entwhistle, 2000). This development is relatable to the distinction between the upper class and the lower class in folk dress displays in the Scandinavian museums. Anne Buck, a British curator who visited museums in Sweden and Denmark in 1939, noted that "the figures used for upper-class costume are headless, while peasant figures have heads" (Buck, 1958). For ethnic robes or folk dresses associated with peasants, the surrounding of these working-class people's habits was also represented so that viewers could imagine an entire household. For upper-class costume, museum visitors were supposed to appreciate an opulent dress as a form of art or to praise the workmanship by focusing on embellishments or ornaments.

As an example of absence of mannequins, I would like to discuss the impact and the legacy of *When Silk Was Gold: Central Asian and Chinese Textiles*, an exhibition held at the Metropolitan Museum of Art in 1997. Sixty-four works from the collections of The Metropolitan Museum of Art and The Cleveland Museum of Art were carefully chosen to present supreme examples of imperial embroidery and weaving workshops of the Middle Ages, from the eighth to the fifteenth century. As its title implies, the exhibition aimed to highlight the importance of luxury textiles in the history of Asian art. For audiences in the United States, curators of the show related the international trade of textiles across Central Asia to fragmentary artifacts found in European church treasuries and royal insignia. They also made an effort to present textiles as a vehicle to disseminate cultural and religious motifs to different ethnic groups. The show was unique in its ambition to present items of the highest quality of luxury. Even though textile examples were abundant and "bodily" statues of Buddhist deities were readily available in many museum collections at the time, curators had hardly tried to place garments or reconstructed garments on the bodies (Palmer, 2008). If they had to, they would use generic types of partial body forms for hats or boots.

In this exhibition, a group of mannequins posed in action was dressed in full suits of armor, sometimes mounted on horse-shaped figures. Curators dressed abstract mannequins with various parts such as helmets, chest plates, skirts, leg guards, and masks covering the entire body from head to toe. As opposed to realistic mannequins, abstract mannequins do not have sculpted details of the facial features, muscles, joints, or fingernails. Instead of utilizing dress forms with armor, these groups in *Samurai!* displayed mannequins walking or leaning forward so that a larger-than-life stature is emphasized

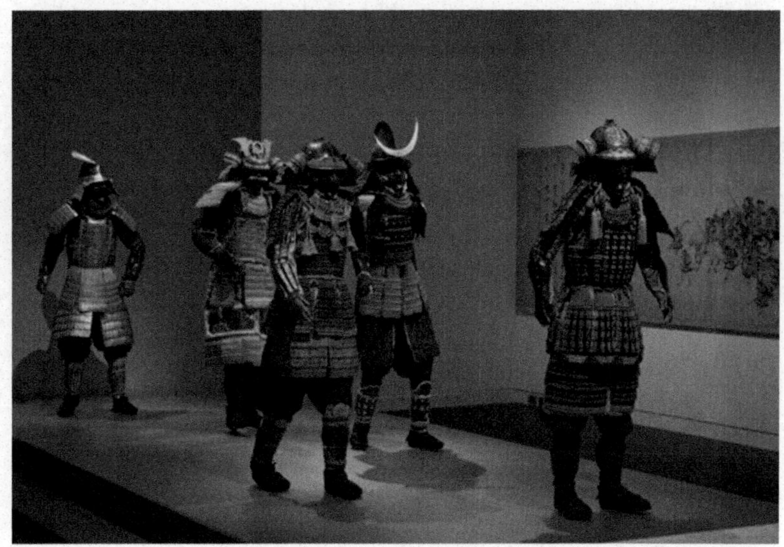

*Figure 5.1* Installation view of *Samurai! Armor from the Ann and Gabriel Barbier-Mueller Collection* (2013), Museum of Fine Arts, Boston.

*Source:* Photograph © Museum of Fine Arts, Boston.

(Figure 5.1). This exhibition is a rarity in art museums. Even though many pieces of Japanese armor are part of permanent displays, few have any sense of movement or active gesture. Tall samurai mannequins also contrasted with boyish, "cute" male models often seen in Japanese and Korean fashion magazines. Monden has argued that magazine culture in Japan seeks to establish the idea that slender, boyish, and sophisticated images of contemporary Japanese men serve as an alternative to the established yet less attractive image of Japanese masculinity as epitomized by worn-out, middle-aged men (Monden, 2015). In my mind, active samurai mannequins in action were more reminiscent of sports mannequins for Nike or Adidas than of stern military leaders of the Kamamura or Muromachi periods.

This conscientious effort to stay away from "life groups" is still prevalent among museum curators. Instead of accurate reconstructions, art museums tend to treat clothing and textile objects as examples of fine art – such as sculpture or painting. *China through the Looking Glass*, a 2015 exhibition at the Metropolitan Museum, was replete with high-fashion slender schläppi mannequins. This choice of display with clothes hung on mannequins positioned on plinths was deliberate in many high-fashion exhibitions as well as in boutiques. Viewers were not encouraged to identify these bodies with those of one particular race, although this practice of using schläppi mannequins is a social statement in which one emphasizes the hegemony of Western haute-couture readiness in bodily proportions.[5]

## From the invisible to the real: rise of Asian fashion and mannequins in art museums

Asian physique shown in mannequins in museums and in retail boutiques is related to the rise of Asian fashion designers in the 1980s. As Yuniya Kawamura has convincingly demonstrated, the emergence of anti-fashion aesthetics by Rei Kawakubo, Junya Watanabe, Kenzo, Issey Miyaki, and Michiko Koshino in London and Paris created a sensational reception of the Asian physique.[6] In the early twenty-first century, the global fashion world has influenced art museums to swing from dress museology to fashion museology as noted by dress historians. Instead of showing historical garments and archaeological textiles with a longer period of conservation and planning, art museums more frequently concentrate on haute-couture designer collections as is shown in *Alexander MacQueen: Savage Beauty* at the V&A Museum, London (2015) or *Rei Kawakubo: Comme des Garçons: Art of the In-Between* at the Metropolitan Museum of Art (2017). In recent exhibitions in Europe and North America, global fashion watchdogs have focused more on the impact of how people get dressed, while art museums focus on designers (Maynard, 2004).

Over 100 years, the three most common types of mannequins are still popular: first, realistic mannequins with faces and hair; second, abstract mannequins with minimalist detail; and third, headless mannequins with a long neck but no head. Based on these stylistic divisions, one can also classify mannequins by function: dress forms known as tailors' dummies with a canvas-covered torso and a wire bottom; ghost mannequins with transparent, movable body parts that are invisible in photography; flexible mannequins made of density foams in elbow, knees, or shoulders for flexible poses; torso mannequins; and standalone mannequin parts for arms, legs, or feet. In one popular website for mannequins for sale, one can find African American mannequins, but not any Asian mannequins.[7] Some stores now carry "museum mannequins," which display mannequins intended for a more didactic and scholarly use. They are meant to display various items of clothing, accessories, and so on from other ages; they depict all sorts of past fashion styles, lifestyles and so on. These museum mannequins can exhibit historical figures and important personalities throughout time, scenes from significant moments in history, war scenes, victories, and many others. Their aim is to provide an accurate image for both scientific and historical means.

Museum mannequins are useful in any museum as they employ storytelling strategies to viewers, especially for younger audiences. To make episodes from the past more entertaining and fascinating, mannequins can be installed as part of historical narratives. They are easy to maneuver, store, and display and they come in all sorts of sizes, styles, and shapes. There are also both female museum mannequins and male museum mannequins, and they can be found in plenty of colors, including multiple skin types as well. As fashion curator Anne-Sofie Hjemdahl stated "how specific bodies produced by museum staff may influence the public's reception of dress and time" (2014).

Marco Centin was the exhibition designer for the *Couture Korea* at the Asian Art Museum in San Francisco. As comparable with any other historical dresses, Korean traditional dresses were made in much smaller sizes than the current smallest adult size, equivalent to European size 36 or American size 00 (Figure 5.2). Also, more women's bodies were needed than men's (Grosz, 1994). Upper-class women's clothing was more readily available for collections and displays than dresses for servants or farmers.[8] This rule also applied to this exhibition. Denis Migdail, the museum conservator who worked with Centin, had to either create custom-made dress forms or use a gas-filled polyethylene bag to give volume to dresses hung over a wire hanger. Also, the display cases were originally installed for hanging scrolls or objects on the pedestal, so cases could not accommodate an adult man's

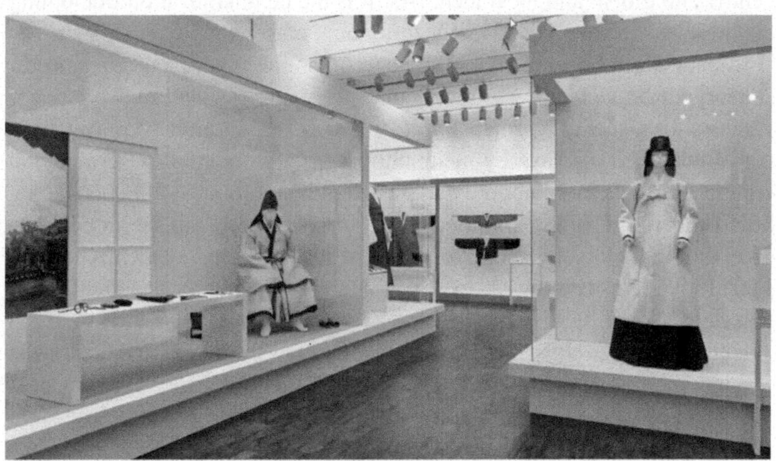

*Figure 5.2* Installation view of *Couture Korea* (2017), Asian Art Museum of San Francisco.

*Source:* Photograph © Asian Art Museum of San Francisco.

stature in mannequins. Thus, Centin and Migdail came up with an idea of a gentleman seated on a stool, which is not quite complying with the custom in a gentleman's studio. Men are either seated on the floor or standing; they would hardly ever squat on a stool.

Dresses and robes at this exhibition were replicas of historical garments from tombs and from Buddhist reliquaries. Some garments were re-created from pictorial representations in painting. In addition, because the exhibition also included a section of contemporary designers' interpretations of traditional dresses, the exhibition designer used schläppi-style boutique mannequins. Wigs were intentionally not used in order to give a sleek look. The designer was clearly aware of the legacy of body figures in the dioramas at anthropological museums. This exhibition was a successful example of interpreting historical dresses in a modern museum environment. Prejudices over Asian physiques, such as the Lolita girls or Kawaii style, were quite well avoided (Monden, 2015).

At the same institution, another exhibition of Asian dresses was held: *Kimono Refashioned*, which premiered at the Newark Museum in 2018 (Morishima, 2018). The Western understanding of Asian clothing was usually considered to be "exotic" or the "other." In recent years, museum curators and exhibition designers have been careful in envisioning Asian clothing less with craft-centered ornaments and more with high fashion. This is partly because exhibiting fashion through broader socio-cultural historical narratives can reveal societal processes as well as contextualize gender and global and local identities. It is the democratization of clothing culture that has paved the way for fashioning museums.

In both exhibitions, curators were careful not to impose any prejudice or stereotypes on viewers. Abstract mannequins and dress forms were major vehicles for historical garments. In *Couture Korea*, curators were considerate of gendered displays by including not only women but also men and children. Julia Petrova not only addresses the importance of understanding how gendered fashion exhibitions are, but also underlines the importance of exhibiting a diversity of dressed experiences: men, women, children, subcultures, etc. (Petrov, 2014). A next step of using mannequins in art museums would be to engage historical objects to convey life stories and personal identities (Pecorari, 2014). On growing visibility of mannequins in fashion exhibitions in art museums, Marie Riegels Melchior's comment is worthy of our attention: "Fashion is eye-catching and as such not just about attracting new visitors, but also attracting media and getting their attention" (Melchior, 2014). The San Francisco Asian Art Museum drew the attention of the media beyond the realm of Asian studies and art museum aficionados in its exhibits. Museums tend to adapt to management strategies to survive by attracting the growing heritage industry and the tourism economy (Svensson, 2014).

In the recent book *Ornamentalism*, Anne A. Cheng, professor of American literature, argued that the West has created an artificial image of Asian women in an extremely decorative and ornate objecthood.[9] That view has often been reflected on exhibition designs and related props such as mannequins.

The Peabody Essex Museum (PEM) recently organized a new exhibition called *Empresses of China's Forbidden City* in 2018–2019 (Wang, 2018), which showed lives of court women during the Qing dynasty. In this exhibition, instead of being dressed on mannequins, imperial robes were hung on garment hangers suspended from the ceiling of the display case. This choice might have been deliberate as there were several portraits of empresses, and the PEM likely wanted to avoid creating a false persona with mannequins. Three empresses were shown in their posthumous portraiture: Empress Dowager Chongqing (1693–1777); Empress Xiaoxian (1712–1748); and Empress Cixi (1835–1908). Similarly, the Diana Exhibition at Kensington Palace in 2017 employed a strategy of displaying multiple portrait images of Princess Diana with her dresses over the faceless body forms or on dress stands with transparent structures.

Around the same time, the Metropolitan Museum of Art had a large-scale exhibition called the *Tale of Genji: A Japanese Classic Illustrated* on the *Genji monogatari*, a classic novel from the eleventh century written by a court lady, Murasaki Shikibu. The story is deeply embedded in the courtly splendor of the Heian period of Japan, so the curator included a mannequin that resembled a noble prince, Hikaru Genji. Standing in a period room reconstructed with the tatami floor and bamboo window hangings, the tall, slender mannequin without the facial features matched the proportions of Prince Genji in many illustrated narrative scenes as told in various passages throughout the novel. He was often praised for his sensitive choice of colors matching seasonal festivities. Nonetheless, there was not much information provided on the choice of garment and headgear on the mannequin even though they were both replicas of historical dress.

For the exhibition *Items: Is Fashion Modern?* held at the Museum of Modern Art in 2017–2018, curators used a mixture of dress forms without heads; suit hangers; faceless head forms; and full mannequins without hair. The show was a more clinical version of garments as objects or specimens rather than reconstruction of historical contexts. For displaying the headscarves of West Asian countries, faceless head forms wrapped with the cloth were employed to look universal and anonymous. However, a video demonstration in a tablet monitor in front of the display added cultural contexts to these headgears in regards to who wears headscarves and how they are worn.

A decade later, *Orientalism: Visions of the East in Western Dress* was envisioned by Costume Institute curators Richard Martin and Harold Koda in 1994. This exhibit was an application of Asian dresses to the Euro-American fashion boutiques. Later, Harold Koda's *Extreme Beauty: Body Transformed* (2001) featured the striking examples of fashionable customs such as foot binding and caged nails of the Manchu noble women of the Qing dynasty along with men's corsets of Europe and neck-extending chokers of the Maasai. There was no reference to the Asian physique in mannequins, as these shows aimed at displaying abstract qualities such as creativity and imagination. A similar tendency of installing a "spectacular" exhibition was criticized in *Fashion India: Spectacular Capitalism* held in the Historical Museum, Oslo in 2013–2014. Teresa Kuldova, the curator and the exhibition designer of the show, acknowledged problematizing the contemporary museum practice of presenting clothing in a spectacular form with accentuated lighting and display furniture over content and prioritizing designers and their creativity over collaborative work in the hierarchies of power (2014).

Ironically, the most realistic life-sized "mannequins" in art museums were not mannequins for dresses but substitutes of real people in observance of the ancient funerary practices – the terracotta warriors of the Han dynasty. *Age of Empires: Chinese Art of the Qin and Han Dynasties (221 BC – AD 220)* featured a dozen statues of Qinshihuangdi's terracotta warriors, lent by Emperor Qinshihuang's Mausoleum Site Museum. These standing figures are over 198 centimeters tall and 70 centimeters wide in the shoulders. This arrangement of terracotta warriors was also prominent in the Guggenheim Museum's *China, 5000 Years: Innovation and Transformation in the Arts*, which was held twenty years ago in 1998.[10] The difference between the two exhibitions was that *Age of Empires* brought a larger group of terracotta statues either in action or in movement along with a chariot.

In the postcolonial era of cross-cultural representations, curators and exhibition designers should critically examine the impact of racial formation in US society as reflected in heritage preservation, popular culture, visual culture, and the domain of contemporary art. They must critique and break down the complex and often contested category of "Asian Civilizations" as well as of "Asian Americans" away from Eurocentric narrative of history writing, as is argued by Christina Kreps and Joy Hendry (Kreps, 2003). Eventually, they should be able to identify the characteristics and perspectives of major movements and thematic trends in representation – visual, literary, and material – of historical people in various countries in Asia as well as Asian American immigration history. With the rise of robotics and artificial intelligence, mannequins will evolve into something more "authentic" and impactful than fiberglass human forms.

## Notes

1 There was a brief moment of surrealist exhibitions with realistic mannequins as shown in Man Ray, Salvador Dalí, and Marcel Duchamp, as discussed in Lewis Kachur, *Displaying the Marvelous: Marcel Duchamp, Salvador Dalí, and Surrealist Exhibition Installations* (Cambridge, MA: The MIT Press, 2003). Schiaparelli also used masks and mannequins in the 1930s. See Caroline Evans, "Masks, Mirrors and Mannequins: Elsa Schiaparelli and the Decentered Subject," *Fashion Theory* 3, no. 1 (1999): 3–31. As the rise of abstract expressionism and minimalism has become prevalent, department stores also swung away from realistic mannequins to abstract ones. Caroline Evans, "Jean Patou's American Mannequins: Early Fashion Shows and Modernism," *Modernism/Modernity* 15, no. 2 (2008): 243–263. https://muse.jhu.edu/ (accessed June 22, 2019); and Rudi Laermans, "Learning to Consume: Early Department Stores and the Shaping of the Modern Consumer Culture (1860–1914)," *Theory, Culture & Society* 10, no. 4 (November 1993): 79–102.

2 Folk museums or historical museums employed realistic mannequins and dioramas during the military dictatorship in Asian countries or for the social realism in China and North Korea. See a case study of the Taiwanese National History Museum in Marzia Varutti, "Materializing the Past: Mannequins, History and Memory in Museums: Insight from the Northern European and East-Asian Contexts," *Nordisk Museologi*, Theme Section: Bodyworks (2017): 5–20. Benjamin P. Birdwhistell, "Manipulated Museum History and Silenced Memories of Aggression: Historical Revisionism and Japanese Government Censorship of Peace Museums," M.A. thesis, University of New Orleans, New Orleans, 2017 discussed a compromise imposed on peace museums using mannequins and simulacra to emphasize Japanese victimization over Japanese aggression during World War II.

3 For example, see exhibitions or writings by Jerome Silbergeld, Sherman E. Lee, and other major scholars of Asian art. Major publications on Asian art from the 1960s to the 1980s focus on painting, calligraphy, and sculpture. Chae-wŏn Kim and Wonyong Kim, *Treasures of Korean Art: 2000 Years of Ceramics, Sculpture, and Jeweled Arts* (New York: Harry N. Abrams, 1966); Jerome Silbergeld, "Chinese Painting Studies in the West: A State-of-the-Field Article," *The Journal of Asian Studies* 46, no. 4 (1987): 849–897; René Yvon Lefebvre d'Argencé, ed., *Treasures from the Shanghai Museum: 6,000 Years of Chinese Art* (San Francisco: Asian Art Museum, 1983); Sherman E. Lee, *Japanese Screens from the Museum and Cleveland Collections* (Cleveland: The Museum, 1977); Laurence C. S. Sickman and Alexander Coburn Soper, *The Art and Architecture of China* (Harmondsworth, Eng.: Penguin Books, 1971).

4 See some early exhibitions on Asian clothing in North American museums: Alan Priest and Pauline Simmons, *Chinese Textiles: An Introduction to the Study of Their History, Sources, Technique, Symbolism, and Use* (New York: The Metropolitan Museum of Art, 1934); Alan Priest, *Costumes from the Forbidden City* (New York: The Metropolitan Museum of Art, 1945); Helen Elizabeth Fernald, *Chinese Court Costumes* (Toronto: Royal Ontario Museum of Archaeology,

1946); Verity Wilson and Ian Thomas, *Chinese Dress* (London: Victoria and Albert Museum, 1986); Shigeki Kawakami and Yoko Woodson, *Classical Kimono from the Kyoto National Museum: Four Centuries of Fashion* (San Francisco: Asian Art Museum; Seattle: distributed by University of Washington Press, 1997).

5 See an interview with Valerie Steel by Matthew Linde in "A Vogue Idea: Dress, Body & Culture/Valerie Steel," *Flash Art*, September 6, 2016. https://flash art.com/2016/09/dress-body-culture-valerie-steele/ (accessed June 13, 2019). Read more about her view in Valerie Steele, "The Corset: Fashion and Eroticism," *Fashion Theory*: *The Journal of Dress, Body & Culture* 3 (1999): 449–473.

6 Yuniya Kawamura, *The Japanese Revolution in Paris Fashion* (London: Bloomsbury Academic, 2006). She analyzes three cases: Kenzo; Rei Kawakubo, Issey Miyake, and Yohji Yamamoto; Hanae Mori.

7 Among many mannequin shopping sites, see www.mannequinmall.com (accessed June 16, 2019).

8 In the periods when museums were dominated by dress museology, upper-class women's fashion was in focus.

9 Anne Anlin Cheng, *Ornamentalism* (Oxford: Oxford University Press, 2019), pp. 1–23; esp. p. 2: "We have yet to look closely at the strange figuration of the yellow woman because she/it stirs up a set of embattled issues that have always haunted feminism: the distressing affinity that can exist between agency and complicity, anti essentialism and authenticity, and affirmation and reification." In the book, Cheng discussed *China through the Looking Class*, an exhibition held at the Metropolitan Museum in 2015 from a feminist and revisionist perspective.

10 Zhixin Sun et al., eds., *Age of Empires: Chinese Art of the Qin and Han Dynasties (221 B.C. – A.D. 220)* (New York: Metropolitan Museum of Art, 2017) and Sherman E. Lee et al., eds., *China, 5000 Years: Innovation and Transformation in the Arts* (New York: Harry N. Abrams, 1998). It should be worth noting that *Age of Empires* brought artworks depicting diverse ethnic communities in a large territory of the Han dynasty including Central Asia adjacent to the Western Asia. Some of them were not well known in textbooks published before the 1990s.

## References

Buck, Anne. *Costume: A Handbook for Textile Curators* (London: The Museum Association, 1958).

Cheng, Anne Anlin. *Ornamentalism*. Oxford: Oxford University Press, 2019.

Clifford, James. *The Predicament of Culture: Twentieth-Century Ethnography, Literature, and Art* (Cambridge, MA: Harvard University Press, 2002).

Cumming, Valerie, C. W. Cunnington, and P. E. Cunnington, "Mannequin," in *The Dictionary of Fashion History* (Oxford: Berg Publishers, 2010), 127.

Entwistle, Joanne. *The Fashioned Body: Fashion, Dress, and Modern Social Theory* (Cambridge: Polity Press, 2000).

Gould, Stephen J. and Robert N. Stinerock. "Self-Fashioning Oneself Cross-Culturally: Consumption as the Determined and the Determining," in *Advances in Consumer Research*, Volume 19, eds. John F. Sherry, Jr. and Brian Sternthal (Austin, TX: University of Texas and the Association for Consumer Research, 1992), pp. 857–860.

Greczy, Adam. *The Artificial Body in Fashion and Art: Marionettes, Models, and Mannequins*. London: Bloomsbury Academic, 2018.

Greenblatt, Stephen. *Renaissance Self-Fashioning: From More to Shakespeare* (Chicago: University of Chicago Press), p. 2.

Grosz, Elizabeth. *Volatile Bodies: Toward a Corporeal Feminism* (Bloomington, IN: Indiana University Press, 1994).

Hjemdahl, Anne-Sofie. "Exhibiting the Body, Dress, and Time in Museums: A Historical Perspective," in *Fashion and Museums: Theory and Practice*, edited by Marie Riegels Melchior and Birgitta Svensson (London: Bloomsbury Academic, 2014), pp. 108–125. Dress, Body, Culture.

Kreps, Christina. *Liberating Culture: Cross-Cultural Perspectives on Museums, Curation, and Heritage Preservation* (London: Routledge, 2003).

Kuldova, Tereza. "Fashion Exhibition as a Critique of Contemporary Museum Exhibitions: The Case of 'Fashion India: Spectacular Capitalism," *Critical Studies in Fashion & Beauty* 5 no. 2 (2014): 313–336.

Margaret, Maynard. *Dress and Globalization* (Manchester: Manchester University Press, 2004).

Melchior, Marie Riegels, and Brigitta Svensson, eds. *Fashion and Museums: Theory and Practice*. London: Bloomsbury Academic, 2014.

Monden, Masafumi. "*Boy's Elegance: A Liminality of Boyish Charm and Old-World Suavity,*" *in Japanese Fashion Cultures: Dress and Gender in Contemporary Japan* (London: Bloomsbury Academic, 2015), 45–76.

Monden, Masafumi. "*Glacé Wonderland: Cuteness, Sexuality and Young Women,*" *in Japanese Fashion Cultures: Dress and gender in contemporary Japan* (London: Bloomsbury Academic, 2015), 77–106.

Morishima, Yuki, et als., eds., *Kimono Refashioned: Japan's Impact on International Fashion* (San Francisco: Asian Art Museum, 2018).

Palmer, Alexandra. "Untouchable: Creating Desire and Knowledge in Museum Costume and Textile Exhibitions." *Fashion Theory*: *The Journal of Dress, Body & Culture* 12 (2008): 31–63.

Pecorari, Marco. "*Contemporary Fashion History in Museums,*" *in Fashion and Museums: Theory and Practice*, ed. Marie Riegels Melchior and Birgitta Svensson (London: Bloomsbury Academic, 2014), 46–60.

Petrov, Julia. "*Gender Considerations in Fashion History Exhibitions*" *in Fashion and Museums: Theory and Practice*, ed. Marie Riegels Melchior and Birgitta Svensson (London: Bloomsbury Academic, 2014), 77–90.

Sandberg, Mark. *Living Pictures, Missing Persons*: *Mannequins, Museums and Modernity*. Princeton, NJ: Princeton University Press, 2003.

Steele, Valerie. "A Museum of Fashion Is More Than a Clothes-Bag." *Fashion Theory*: *The Journal of Dress, Body & Culture* 2 (1998): 327–336.

Svensson, Birgitta. "In Conclusion: Museums Dressed in Fashion," in *Fashion and Museums: Theory and Practice*, edited by Marie Riegels Melchior and Birgitta Svensson (London: Bloomsbury Academic, 2014), pp. 197–205.

Wang, Yiyou, et als., *Empresses of China's Forbidden City: 1644–1912* (Salem, MA: Peabody Essex Museum, 2018).

# 6 Figures of speech

## Black History at the National Great Blacks in Wax Museum

*Bridget R. Cooks*

In 1983, husband and wife team Elmer P. Martin and Joanne Mitchell Martin co-founded The Martins' Wax Exhibition of Great Afro-Americans, a traveling exhibit in Baltimore, Maryland. The idea for a museum fulfilled the two young educators' dream of finding a way to involve the Baltimore community, particularly African American youth, with Afrocentric principals that value knowledge and pride about Black history. They chose the re-creation of the human form as the vehicle for developing an immersive educational experience. The placement of figures in compartmentalized spaces with contextual clues makes the museum unlike any other wax or African American museum.

What started as a mobile and interactive display of four notable figures has grown into a national institution with over 150. For the past decade, the museum, known now as the National Great Blacks in Wax Museum, has been the most attended museum of any kind in the state of Maryland (National Great Blacks in Wax Museum). It is a singular place of reflection for the community and hosts visitors from across the globe. The museum's use of life-size mannequins, wax figures, and sculptures expresses the urgency of knowing Black history through personal encounters and collective identity. Further, its location within an economically impoverished part of the city underscores the importance of having cultural knowledge to understand and transform systems of power. The combination of figurative-based content within the socio-economic context of Baltimore allows Great Blacks in Wax to present narratives of Black survival and accomplishment *through* material conditions of poverty and oppression. In this way, the impact of the museum content is all the more profound. Visitors are not removed from daily reality to experience exhibitions that promote fairy tale narratives of Black progress. Instead, they find moments of violence, trauma, and celebration – a cycle that resonates with the current conditions of Black life they encounter when they leave the museum.

DOI: 10.4324/9780429260575-6

Several events inspired the Martins to establish the museum. First, in 1978, Elmer Martin was a new professor of social work at Morgan State University, a public historically Black research university in Baltimore where he taught classes about Black families, communities, and mental health. His pedagogical approach was steeped in ideologies of Black purposefulness that at the time was central to the recent Black Power movement. Yet, he was surprised that his students did not share his Afrocentric perspective. The students believed that showing pride in their race would keep them from succeeding in the workplace. They wanted to learn about topics that were deemed valuable in American mainstream culture. Confused by the younger generation's preference for White assimilation over narratives of Black pride, Martin concluded that Black people had failed to institutionalize the significance of Black history. This he set out to change (Martin, interview).

Simultaneously, Martin sponsored a little league baseball team in Baltimore. Each player was required to have a photo identification card as proof of team membership. One young player rejected his photograph and demanded that Martin make the photographer retake his picture because he perceived himself as looking "too Black." Martin questioned what "too Black" meant and asked himself why Blackness was being rejected after the age of Black power. Looking back on this moment recently, Joanne Martin commented, "It's taken a while to get from the point of, 'I'm Black and I'm Proud' to 'Black Lives Matter.' Our plan with the museum was to get past this idea of rejecting our Blackness. We aren't there even today."[1]

The Martins were determined to create something to empower the next generation. They had little money, but they had education.[2] In 1978, the couple published the first of several co-authored books about social work and Black American communities.[3] These publications allowed them to reach a small scholarly audience; however, the books did not reach the youth. Elmer's mantra was: "Community development and cultural development go hand in hand. Conventional wisdom all over this nation is that you hide your poverty areas. Once you succeed in hiding them, you can succeed in neglecting them" (Martin, interview). Black visibility was key for the Martins' goal to develop their community through the tradition of cultural uplift.

An impressive family trip to Potter's Wax Museum in St. Augustine, Florida helped the Martins put their ideas of Black empowerment into action. Founded in 1949, Potter's features wax figures of characters from popular films, athletes, and politicians. "Blown away" by the Potter's replicas of historical figures and entertainers, the Martins were inspired to create figures of Black people to educate and edify their audience (Martin, interview). Their research into the relationship between visual objects, history, and community building led them to visit England, France, and Spain where they were impressed by the functions of public monuments to define history and national identity. They were particularly moved by The London Dungeon, because it focused on the cruel mindset of English people who deliberately tortured and murdered others to express their ability to control. Inhumane treatment and its horrible effects were matters of fact that the Martins wanted to convey through their exhibitions. Likewise, visits to the Cherokee Museum in North Carolina and the Museum of Tolerance in Los Angeles were influential in the educational and emotional dimensions they imagined for their wax museum. Through figurative displays, the Martins would create a place to defy anyone who claimed that Black people did not belong in America. Further, they would resist the pressure to "pretty up" Black history and not tell the truth of struggle, survival, and accomplishment (Martin, interview).

## The Martins' wax exhibition of great Afro-Americans

Elmer developed his talent for sculpture through classes at the Maryland Institute College of Art (MiCA) and Morgan State University. As a figurative sculptor, Elmer had faith that three-dimensional objects could make an incomparable impact on viewers. Joanne remembers that he would say, "You can put a wax figure across a room and people are going to naturally gravitate to it in a way that a piece of art or a document would not. The minute they ask the question 'Who is that?' or 'What is that?' Then you'll be in the position to teach. It is a combination of those things. It's creating a desire to know" (Martin, interview). The Martins had the artistic skill, commitment to community, and desire to educate. However, starting a wax museum was an entirely new endeavor. They started their project with help from Rob Dorfman, a second-generation wax figure maker based in Baltimore. The Martins' first commission of personages from Dorfman were educator Mary McLeod Bethune, abolitionist and American ambassador Frederick Douglass, radical abolitionist John Brown, and slave rebellion leader Nat Turner. They were convinced that these four legendary American heroes would capture the attention of their desired audience by tapping into the community's desire for knowledge about Black history. Within the first two years of operation, the Martins and their growing crew of historical characters had outgrown the space needed to accommodate the thousands of visitors that visited from the city and across the Eastern Seaboard.

The figures were displayed in a shotgun house on Saratoga Street, and the Martins regularly traveled with them for exhibitions at schools, churches, and malls. These community spaces allowed the Martins to reach visitors who were not aware of the project called The Martins' Wax Exhibition of Great Afro-Americans and to test the level of enthusiasm about a future museum. The primary purpose of the exhibitions was educational, and viewers showed their commitment to supporting the Martins' work by leaving money in the lap of Bethune's dress.

The exhibition of the first figures addressed the Martins' educational and personal goals. Joanne recalls learning about Black people as a child through Negro History Week. When the week was over, the discussion was also. For her, the protagonists and their stories were abstract without images to make the people seem real. The museum project was a response to her inability to understand the significance of those weeks. She says, "These wax figures put a face on history" (Martin, interview). Encouraged by the enthusiasm of their visitors, the Martins expanded their space to reach more people. In 1988, they moved the exhibition to a 15,000 square foot decommissioned firehouse on 1601 E. North Avenue located in Oliver, a predominantly Black community in east Baltimore that persists through economic blight. The Martin's Wax Exhibition of Great Afro-Americans then became the National Great Blacks in Wax Museum, a multi-leveled exhibition hall with dioramas illustrating historical moments that recreate people and scenes from the Middle Passage through the twenty-first century. The collection of inspirational replicants are the primary means of connecting audiences with living and ancestral icons.

With more space came a purposeful set of objectives:

1. To stimulate an interest in African American history by revealing the little-known, often-neglected facts of history.
2. To use great leaders as role models to motivate youth to achieve.
3. To improve race relations by dispelling myths of racial inferiority and superiority.
4. To support and work in conjunction with other nonprofit, charitable organizations seeking to improve the social and economic status of African Americans.

(National Great Blacks in Wax Museum)

These goals are reached through a series of exhibitions dedicated to individual figures and themes. Docents activate the space through tours that address local, national, and African histories. The Great Blacks in Wax Museum is a place that has to be visited to be believed. It combines the drama of theatrical settings with stories of triumph and the macabre. It stands as a refuge and place of validation and education for the community.

## Materiality

The Martins' first purchase from Dorfman marked the beginning of their learning curve for populating the museum. Made from a composite of wax and vinyl, complete bodies are expensive. The Martins soon learned that the same lifelike effect can be achieved by constructing the clothed parts of the body with more affordable materials such as chicken wire. Benefitting from some success, the couple added to their collection by purchasing nineteen mannequins and mannequin parts from a department store that was going out of business. They also commissioned sculptors to create the faces of particular people and used repurposed materials to form the bodies. Their eclectic "make do" resourcefulness allowed for a variety of representational styles to create a visually heterogeneous collection.

Each type of material – wax, vinyl, ceramic sculpture, and plastic mannequins – has a different effect. Although advanced techniques were used to make the original four figures appear realistic (the teeth of the figures are made from dental acrylic used for dentures, and the facial hair is punched in one strand at a time), Joanne finds that they lack the lifelike vibrancy of the forms added in the last several years (Martin, interview). More recently acquired figures, such as the representation of educator Carter G. Woodson who greets visitors in the museum lobby, is made entirely of beeswax, making his skin look more luminous and humanlike (Figure 6.1). The downside of this radiant quality is that the form is easily breakable. Woodson stands beside an older mannequin form of sociologist and activist W.E.B. DuBois. Positioned behind a column-like podium, each figure looks dignified in a suit and tie, each holding in his hands the biographical text that identifies him. In addition to educating visitors about the historical figures, the pair illustrates the evolution of figures in the museum. A comparison between the two shows more realistic skin texture, color, and hair for Woodson. The Woodson figure is more easily identifiable as Woodson than DuBois, whose body appears slightly shrunken and discolored. Viewers need to rely on the blue NAACP ribbon pinned to DuBois' jacket and the didactic information to identify him. The range in fidelity to the historical person exemplified by Woodson and DuBois is both economic and deliberate. Martin clarifies that she doesn't want every mannequin to have the smooth skin of the beeswax forms like Woodson. She likes having the slightly flawed quality of the DuBois character beside Woodson because living people have variations in skin texture, hair, and color.

In another example, the original Mary McLeod Bethune figure is less realistic than the more recent rendition. However, when the Martins toured the figures in community spaces, viewers liked the original McLeod Bethune not because it looked just like the educator, but because it reminded them of their grandmothers. Feeling a fondness for a woman of a certain age, shape, and dress made viewers believe in the Martins' project and support the museum. In this way, a mannequin's success is not solely defined by how much it looks like the person it simulates but can involve familiarity and

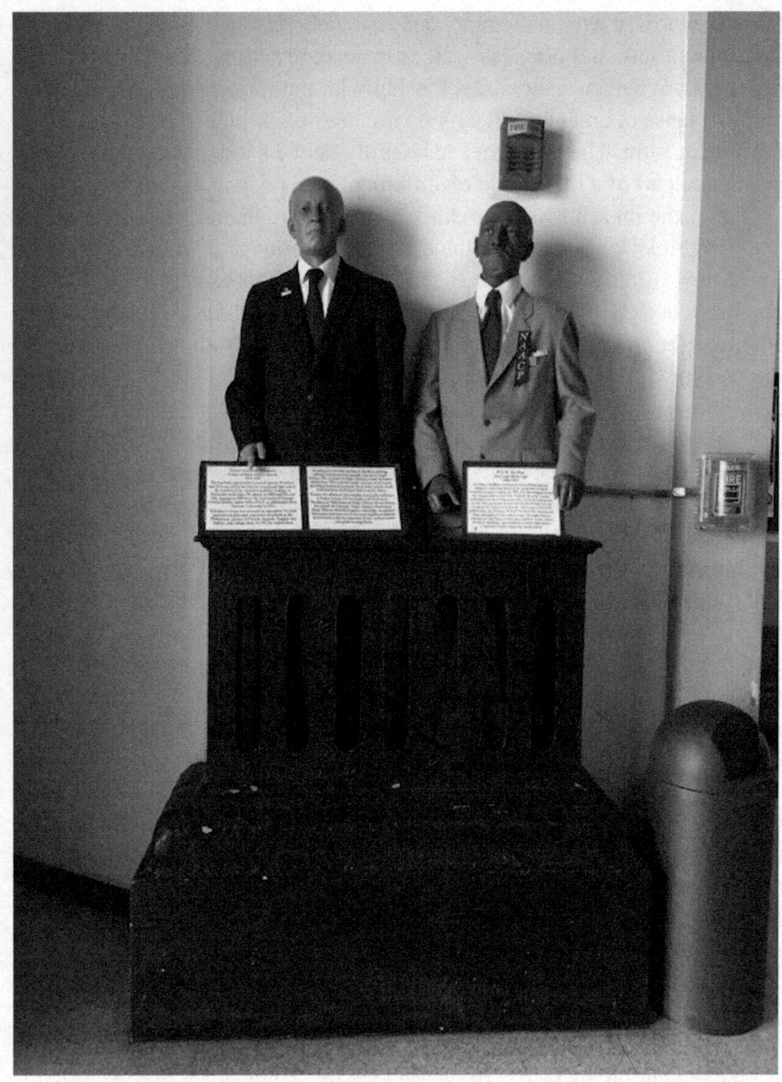


*Figure 6.1* Figures of Carter G. Woodson and W.E.B. DuBois in the lobby of the National Great Blacks in Wax Museum.

*Source:* Photo courtesy of the National Great Blacks in Wax Museum, Inc., Baltimore, Maryland. Photo credit: Bridget R. Cooks.

recognition in ways that are not related to the specific individual represented. In other words, a personal connection to the object may be facilitated by its shape, materials, and dress, as well as its recognizability as the individual it represents. Whether visitors feel kinship with the characters in the museum or not, a sense of urgency and passion is conveyed through the immediacy of the human form. The museum successfully delivers the message that Black people are part of a long cycle of suffering, survival, and achievement.

One of the museum's latest exhibits presents figures of Sojourner Truth and Frederick Douglass under the banner "Abolition and Women's Rights." These new forms demonstrate Joanne's strategic approach to re-presenting popular icons. Her goal was to present Truth, a well-known minister and advocate for women's rights, in an unexpected way. Truth is molded standing and looking up with her arms positioned as if swaying with a natural gait. She is modestly dressed in white but does not wear the white bonnet that she wears in most historical portraits of her. The fidelity of the facial features makes Truth visually recognizable in the wax form and therefore allowed Martin some license to present her in a different fashion. As Martin explained, "People all know the image of old Sojourner Truth sitting with the bonnet on her head. This version changes your comfort zone a little" (Martin, interview). For the new Frederick Douglass, Martin wanted to focus on the quality of the orator's hair texture so that its appearance would evoke natural Black hairstyles today. In this way Douglass presents as a man who continues to be relevant in our times, the result of Martin's decision to change an element of a historical figure's form to pique the interest of visitors to the museum.

The museum receives the most criticism from visitors for its figure of Reverend Martin Luther King, Jr. The Martins chose to depict King in his twenties to remind viewers that he was only twenty-six when he led the Montgomery Bus Boycott in 1956. Shown at this age, visitors don't recognize King. They find immediate recognition and comfort in seeing the civil rights leader in his most reproduced photographic portrait taken by *New York Times* photographer Alan Baum. The photograph has been reproduced on Black church fans for decades. Taken in 1963 when King was 37 years old, Martin states that Baum's photograph of King "shows the weight of the movement on his face." To please visitors, the museum may eventually have two King figures, but Joanne prefers the message at the core of the decision to show the younger King.

Martin prefers to work with different sculptors because she likes incorporating the different interpretations of each artist. The figures are sourced from workshops located all over the country. Specialists contribute different body parts to a complete form. The options of different materials are used for different effects throughout the exhibitions.

## Exhibits

The museum consists of three floors presenting more than thirty-five exhibitions. Most of the figures are presented on the main floor in individual and group configurations. More figures are depicted on the second floor where a community fellowship hall is located for programming. In two separate basements are distinctive exhibits: an immersive walk through the re-creation of the hull of a slave ship, and a space dedicated to the history of lynching and drug addiction in Baltimore (Figure 6.2).[4] The individual exhibitions on the upper floors are a mixture of international, national, and local notables from ancient Carthaginian military commander Hannibal, to Morgan State University choir director, Nathan Carter, Maryland griot Mary Carter Smith, and President Barack Obama. Most of the figures are Black, but there are several White figures, from abolitionist Senator Charles Sumner to a hooded Ku Klux Klansman. Setting the stage for the exhibits are a variety of props including a 500 pound bale of cotton, torture devices used during slavery, posters, postcards, furniture, Black Americana, and reproductions of historical photographs. The scale of the exhibits ranges from human to miniature. Glass cabinets on the main and basement levels feature dollhouse furniture and small sculptures to educate visitors about rural life in West Africa, plantation life for the enslaved, objects that Black people invented or redesigned, Black victims of Black murderers in Baltimore, and lynching victim Emmett Till. Some exhibits, such as *The Makings of a Black Stereotype* are not directly connected to any figurative object. Instead, they provide historical context and critical insight into misperceptions of Black people.

Like the presentation of Truth and Douglass, some exhibits are themed. Others, such as the presentation of Black nationalist Marcus Garvey, focus on single individuals positioned beneath a sign announcing their accomplishment. Many exhibits show figures in action demonstrating their achievements. For instance, the Underground Railroad exhibit shows White abolitionist Thomas Garrett struggling on his knees to push the legs of a Black man into a cast iron stove. Viewers can see that the stove leads to a space behind a brick wall where the man is pulled to freedom by Harriet Tubman, a.k.a. "Black Moses," conductor of the Underground Railroad. In another exhibit, the figure of jazz musician and composer James Hubert "Eubie" Blake sits at the keys of a piano while Billie Holiday sings by his side. In the most dynamic of the main floor exhibits, *A Journey to Freedom*, Henry "Box" Brown is represented as an animatronic form. His head lifts the lid of a wooden box marked with the destination "Philadelphia, PA Adams Express" to peep out at freedom in the North and wave his right hand, assuring viewers of his safe arrival. In front of this scene

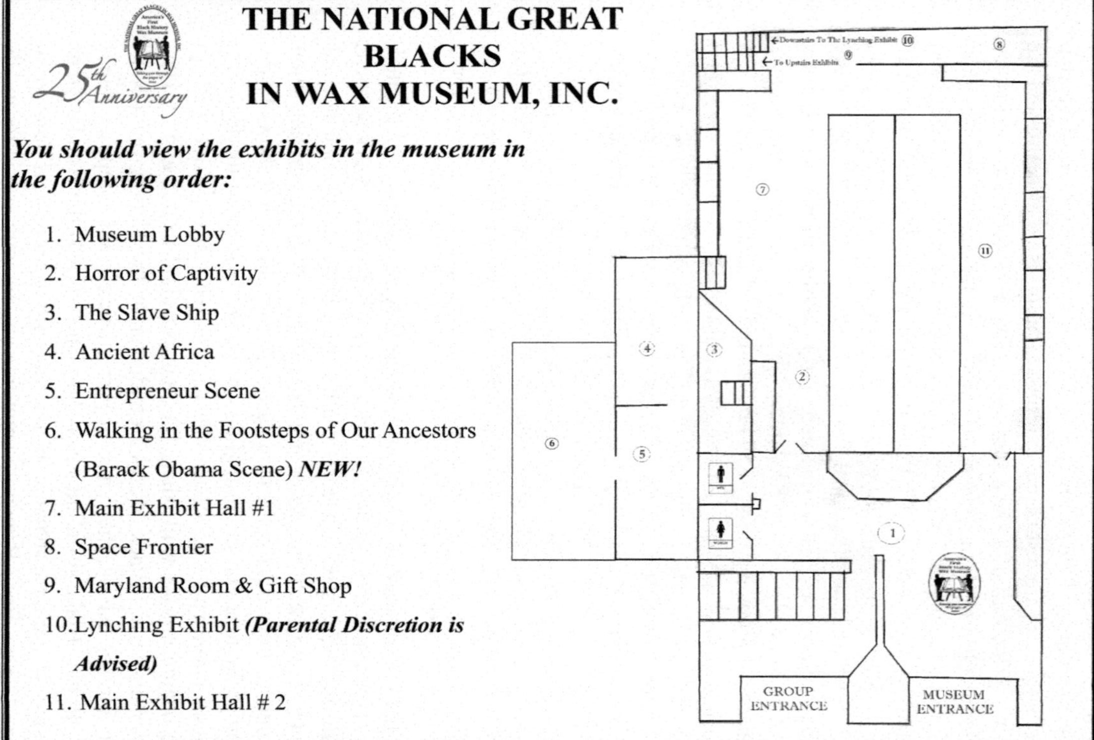


*Figure 6.2* Layout map and recommended viewing route of the National Great Blacks in Wax Museum.

*Source:* Courtesy of the National Great Blacks in Wax Museum, Inc., Baltimore, Maryland.

of the perpetual escape from slavery is a brightly painted lawn jockey. The statue celebrates the terror induced "loyalty" of the enslaved who chose death rather than defy the wishes of a White master. However, placed in the context of the exhibit, the statue's presence seems to honor the bravery of Brown by gesturing toward the fugitive slave.

Perhaps the most memorable exhibit in the museum is the re-creation of the hull of a transatlantic slave ship, part of the exhibition devoted to the Middle Passage. The decision to create the exhibit was critical to the museum's educational mission. It was also informed by a special research trip to Liverpool, England, the most profitable European port for trading human cargo in the eighteenth century. After reading an article about slave records that were kept in a warehouse in Liverpool, Elmer and museum exhibition designer, Howard "Gene" Stinnette travelled to Liverpool to see the papers. The warehouse staff that greeted them claimed to have no knowledge of any slave trade records. However, a Black janitor working nearby overheard their request and interrupted the exchange to confirm that the visitors were in the correct place. Elmer's goal for the visit to the archives was to find first-person narratives by people who were directly involved in the trade. After returning to Baltimore, these voices would become part of the exhibit in text and audio to tell the stories of enslavement through personal testimonies.

Visitors approach *The Middle Passage* exhibit by walking alongside the re-creation of the ship through the Horror of Captivity area (number 2 on the map, Figure 6.2). On the ship's deck above, two mannequins of sailors in red and white striped shirts stand with a mast, sail, ropes, and net. Using text excerpted from a 1788 diary by slave ship captain Alexander Falconbridge, a sign titled "Forced Dancing" informs viewers that the deck was used to exercise the Africans. Another sign provides information on "The Inspection" by Falconbridge and slave ship captain William Bosman in 1623. Each describes the process of accepting and rejecting Africans for enslavement. Both decisions were followed by violence: beheading for the rejected and branding for the accepted. To the right of the entryway a sign with an explanation of why African captives were thrown overboard is accompanied by the mannequin form of a bloodied African man hanging upside down with shackled hands. Below his hands, the floor is textured and painted blue to represent the ocean. Miniature sharks circle a disembodied dark brown hand that reaches out of a red section of water.

Nearby is an exhibit of two white sailors forcing food into the mouth of a mannequin of a Black man, shackled and bent backwards on his knees. On the wall behind them is an enlarged photograph known as "The Scourged Back" showing the keloid scars of fugitive slave Peter, a.k.a. Gordon, who escaped from captivity in 1863. The image is paired with a display case that contains an actual branch of a cotton plant grown in North Carolina. A few feet away is a mannequin of a Black woman wearing work clothes enclosed by a torturous tracking device around her waist and neck.

The walk into *The Slave Ship* takes visitors downstairs into a narrow basement space (number 3 on the map, Figure 6.2). Upon descent, visitors first encounter two interracial exhibits showing violent acts used regularly to dehumanize Africans and process them as cargo. The first shows three mannequins. A clothed White slaver brands the bloodied shoulder of a screaming Black woman who struggles naked on the ground (Figure 6.3). Beside them is an enslaved Black man standing with his hands trapped in a pillory. The second exhibit titled *Women's Quarters* shows one naked White man who sits in front of three Black women behind vertical bars. The naked woman pushes the man away with her outstretched arm. The other modestly dressed women sit nearby in helpless anticipation of a similar fate. "The Raping of the Women" text panel provides excerpts from first-person accounts of crewmen ritually raping African girls on the ships. These figurative exhibits are supported by a map of trade routes between Europe, Africa, and the Americas, and a collection of reproduced torture and punishment devices called "Tools of the Slave Trade." This exhibit includes the

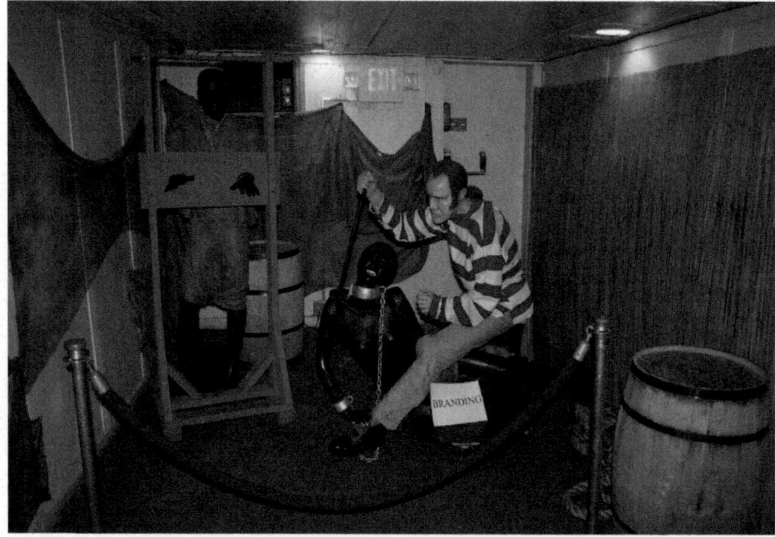


*Figure 6.3* The "Branding" Exhibit at The National Great Blacks in Wax Museum.

*Source:* Photo courtesy of the National Great Blacks in Wax Museum, Inc., Baltimore, Maryland. Photo credit: Huey Copeland.

feature “Beheading as a Means of Control,” which is illustrated by a bloody mannequin head fixed on top of a barrel on the floor.

The positioning of mannequins in each scene effectively conveys the sickening and deeply disturbing subject matter. At the same time, the reality of the museum environment is a reminder of the twenty-first century context. The mannequin displays and their supporting props do not completely obscure the practical setting of the museum. Although viewers likely dismiss the presence of objects such as an air conditioning unit, cardboard boxes, carpet, and decorative fencing from their understanding of the exhibition themes, those objects are part of the museum experience. Making these everyday objects visible generates a greater appreciation for the urgency of the museum’s purpose to convey historical truths of anti-Black rituals and Black survival by helping visitors connect the trauma of the past to the material conditions of the present. In many cases, the unseemly exhibits reject an aesthetically pleasing display of anti-Black violence and instead maintain a crude and uncomfortable presentation that is rooted in the subject matter.

The main part of *The Middle Passage* is divided into sections labeled “Refuse Slaves,” “Sick & Dying Slaves,” “Men’s Quarters,” and “Boy’s Quarters” located along one side of the room length. Mannequins representing each group are displayed in a range of forms from full and half body, to disembodied legs primarily visible by the bottoms of their feet. They are either naked or partially clothed with burlap and chained to silver-colored paper representing thick metal collars, shackles, or manacles. Four forms are fully shrouded in white sheets to represent the dead. The backgrounds of the larger compartments are lined with contemporary enlargements of slavery era prints illustrating the way that Africans were packed into the hull.

The figures in *The Middle Passage* have a different appearance than those that depict famous Black Americans who are honored on the upper floors. The history they illustrate, their various states of undress, and the materials the figures are composed of all contribute to the affective rhetorical power of the exhibit. Dr. Martin explains,

> The majority of what we have is wax figures. However, there is a power to the figures in the slave ship that comes from them not being wax figures. There is almost a crudeness to some of them that conveys the pain. They are posed in certain ways that a wax figure could not be posed. They express the contortion aspects of the slave ship. We wanted mainly mannequins on the slave ship because we could break them apart and show that they were broken bodies that had to hold on to their spirit and their strength. They were people who could not necessarily sit upright. They were packed like spoons in a drawer and books

> on a shelf and those mannequins could help convey that in a way that I really don't think wax figures could.
>
> (Martin, interview)

The halved, broken, and twisted mannequins emphasize the way that the enslavement of Africans depended upon perceiving humans as things. However, the use of customized forms at strategic points injects pathos into the experience that makes a particular connection with visitors. Although the bodies of the Black male figures are mannequins, their faces are all based on one individual. When the exhibition was being conceptualized, Maia Carroll, a woman with experience reconstructing mannequins, chaperoned her son's class visit to the museum. She offered her services to the Martins and was contracted to transform the faces of White mannequins into Black faces. The faces of the boys in the slave ship are all modeled after Carroll's son at different ages (Martin, interview).

The compartments furthest to the right are subtitled "Thirst and Starvation." Half body mannequin forms populate the scene which is described through an 1819 eyewitness account by a slave smuggler named Drake. Two sets of narrow compartments marked "Sickness, Disease, and Death," are divided into six tight shelves with pairs of bodies lying side by side on each row. An 1814 report by British physician Thomas Nelson, who examined Africans upon their arrival to Brazil, explains the slavers' treatment of the ill and dead. The two left compartments present a sculpted figure of a Black man with a pronounced rib cage crumpled on the floor in starvation. Sitting beside him is a life-size sculpture of an elderly man whose whitened eyes indicate blindness. Fingers on his mangled hand are missing. In the compartment below is an abstract figurative form impossibly folded over into a pile of skin and bones. A group of sculpted rats feed on the remains. The body and animals all appear in the same matte black color as if burned to a crisp, emphasizing the horror of death.

The last two compartments show the top halves of two Black male mannequins with defined musculature under the "Refuse Slaves" label. One of the male mannequins looks upward with slightly parted lips providing the first expression of strength and hope in *The Middle Passage*. Duct tape used to fix his broken wrist double as necessary repairs and symbolic shackles. The empty "Guest Quarters" area below gives visitors a space to imagine how they may have faced such a horrible fate. This invitation to the visitor to imagine themself in the Middle Passage is repeated by a room length mirror on the other side of the exhibition space. Doubled by the reflection on the opposite wall, the long wall of male holding cells encompasses viewers and increases the claustrophobic feeling in the windowless basement. At the end of the room, the *Mutiny (Slave Rebellion)* exhibit provides a brief reprieve from the brutality of the previous scenes. Two mannequins of Black men who look like others presented in the compartmental wall are shown using the chains of their shackles to choke a White slaver.

The exhibits on rape, sickness, and death include examples of unique sculptural figures. The most powerful instance of this artistic intervention accompanies the sign "Punishment of Rebellious Slaves." The plaster sculpture of a naked African woman hangs by her bound wrists from a chain. The woman appears unconscious as her head hangs heavy over her back. Her torso bows forward making an arc that swings in the gallery. The appearance of whip lashes into the surface of the sculpture are evidence of the violence enacted on the bodies of enslaved women.[5] The damaged surface reveals the natural wood beneath the brown paint of her skin and marks of bright red paint highlight her suffering. This is clearly not a mannequin. The wholeness of her body, its curves, individual facial features, and size express a vulnerability and accessibility that is unlike any other in the exhibition. She may be one of many Africans like the others in the room. But she is an individual. The difference in her presentation powerfully reminds viewers that all of the Africans were individuals.

The narrow hallway that leads back to the entry staircase is lined with enlarged reproductions of the 1850 daguerreotypes by J.T. Zealy of enslaved people in South Carolina. Commissioned by naturalist and racial scientist Louis Agassiz, the photographs of two women and five men were taken for the purposes of proving that Africans were not human. The legacy of these images has been persistent in anti-Black rhetoric. In the context of *The Middle Passage*, the reproduction of photographs of Renty and Drana are presented as portraits instead of specimens. They are framed in wood and rope threaded with strands of red and green. Displayed under the header "Remember", the images connect the mannequins and sculptures with pictures of actual people who lived through the Middle Passage. The haunting photographs serve as transitional images for visitors to contemplate before ascending to the museum's main floor. Returned to their point of entry, visitors' perception of the wax figures on display throughout the museum may be different than when they first arrived. The achievements that the Great Blacks in Wax signify appear all the more incredible after the exhibitions of violence in *The Slave Ship*.

## Black futures and wax posterity

Since the National Great Black in Wax Museum was founded, wax figures have been added to incorporate people of contemporary relevance and to rethink historical icons, but the museum's permanent exhibits have remained the same. The current arrangement has had a profound influence in art, education, and entertainment. During his artist's residence at the Contemporary Museum in Baltimore, filmmaker Isaac Julien visited Great Blacks in Wax. A few moments into his tour of the museum, he decided that the museum would be featured in his film *Baltimore* (2004). The film tells a history and speculative future of Black Americans through three Baltimore sites: the Walters Art Museum, an encyclopedic museum with art and artifacts from around the world; the National Great Blacks in Wax Museum; and the George Peabody Library that maintains primary holdings in eighteenth and nineteenth-century archaeology and British art and architecture. The wax figure of filmmaker Melvin Van Peebles that was created for the film was acquired by the Studio Museum in Harlem.

As part of the orientation program at Morgan State University, all incoming first year students are required to visit the museum. Implemented in 2012, this initiative brings over 800 students annually through the museum exhibits. When actress Lupita Nyong'o was preparing for her role as Patsey in Steve McQueen's 2013 historical docudrama *Twelve Years a Slave*, she visited Great Blacks in Wax to better understand the history presented in the film (Kaufman, 2013). She was deeply moved by the 500 pound bale of cotton in the main hall, because her character Patsey was rewarded for picking hundreds of pounds of cotton each day.

The relevance and influence of the museum on individual lives is immeasurable. Viewers' personal experiences have impacted thousands of others through the work they were inspired to make because of the museum. Martin has plans to expand the museum to occupy the entire block of 1600 East North Avenue. She envisions a new space that will accommodate many more figures and visitors and transform the block into a commercial district that she hopes will bring financial prosperity to the community. For now, the Great Blacks in Wax Museum stands as a memorial and testament to the value of Black lives, a powerful reminder that those lives matter.

## Notes

1 Joanne also recalled giving children a tour of the museum's Queen of Sheba. The students teased each other by looking at the figure and saying, "You're Black like that!" The association with Blackness and African-ness in particular was weaponized as an insult (Martin, interview).

2 Elmer earned his doctorate of social work from Case Western University in 1975, and JoAnne was working on a PhD from Howard University.

3 Elmer P. Martin and Joanne Mitchell Martin, *The Black Extended Family* (Chicago: University of Chicago Press, 1978), *Helping Tradition in the Black Family and Community* (Washington, D.C., National Association of Social Workers, 1985), *Social Work and the Black Experience* (Washington, D.C., National Association of Social Workers Press, 1995), *Spirituality and the Black Helping*

*Tradition in Social Work* (Washington, D.C., National Association of Social Workers Press, 2003); Joanne Mitchell Martin and Elmer P. Martin, eds., *Prayers of Great Blacks: Frederick Douglass, W.E.B. DuBois, Marcus Garvey, Martin Luther King, Jr., the Hon. Elijah Muhammad, Sojourner, Truth, Harriet Tubman* (Baltimore, Great Blacks in Wax Publication, 1984); Martin and Martin, *The Helping Tradition in the Black Family and Community*.

4 Two publications by artist and literary scholar, Marcus Wood, discuss the museum's strategies for representing the transatlantic slave trade in relationship to other museums (Wood, 2008, 2009). He also includes analyses of the museum's lynching exhibition.

5 Carroll explains that the sculpture "was done with an additive process using plaster, so I would focus on different sections of her body and as I built them up, I would just make a slash. I did not even stop to think about it" (Wood, 2008).

## Bibliography

Kaufman, Amy. "Lupita Nyong'o, the Level-Headed Breakout Star of '12 Years a Slave'." *South Florida Sun Sentinel*, October 23, 2013. <www.sun-sentinel.com/features/celebrity/la-et-lupita-nyongo-20131023-story.html>

Martin, Joanne. Interview by Bridget R. Cooks, September 6, 2018. Baltimore, Maryland.

The National Great Blacks in Wax Museum. "Explore our Past, Plan Our Future." <www.greatblacksinwax.org/expansion_plans.htm>

Wood, Marcus. "Atlantic Slavery and Traumatic Representation in Museums: The National Great Blacks in Wax Museum as a Test Case." *Slavery and Abolition* 29, no. 2 (June 2008): 151–171.

Wood, Marcus. "Slavery, Memory, and Museum Display in Baltimore: The Great Blacks in Wax and the Reginald F. Lewis." *Curator* 51, no. 2 (January 2009): 147–167.

# 7 Black is the color of my true love's skin

## The symbolism and significance of the Black female mannequin figure in Mary Sibande's creative work

*Lanisa S. Kitchiner*

### Introduction

This chapter analyzes how South African artist Mary Sibande uses mannequins to advance new ways of representing Black women in contemporary art. It examines select pieces from her exhibition *Long Live the Dead Queen* (2010), making a two-fold argument that the artworks bestow Black women with agency and disrupt dominant readings of Black female imagery in post-apartheid South Africa and in the art world writ large. The chapter contextualizes Sibande's work within the historical milieu of Black South African domestic worker imagery. It then introduces the limits of academic discourse in interpreting Sibande's mannequin figures. The article draws upon and advances Salah Hassan's concept of insertion to pinpoint how Sibande uses autobiography to animate the human lay figure. There is pervasive reliance on Black feminist thought as a critical interpretive tool throughout the chapter.

Sibande's creations have won local praise and widespread international acclaim. However, critical analyses largely interpret the mannequins in her work as trivial display props for richly symbolic Victorian dresses. In contrast, this chapter recognizes the Black mannequins in Sibande's artistry as multifaceted, hyper-performative communicative devices that conjure problematic histories and persistent challenges of race and representation, spectacle and surveillance, presence and absence. I critique Sibande's mannequins in effort to fill a burgeoning void in scholarship on her work. The premise is that meaning exists not only in and through the elaborate dresses that frame Sibande's figures but also in and through the deliberately blackened skin of her mannequin forms. I contend that the mannequins are doubly charged in South Africa, where images of Black women are often playgrounds of gross fantasy and horrific fetish that bleed between the creative imaginary, intellectual discourse, and the national hermeneutics of rainbowism, recovery, and redress.

DOI: 10.4324/9780429260575-7

## Contextualizing Sophie's radical presence

Mary Sibande debuted Sophie, a hyper-realistic, semi-autobiographical figurative sculpture of a Black female maidservant in her 2009 exhibition, *Long Live the Dead Queen*, at Gallery MOMO in Johannesburg, South Africa. Cast in Sibande's own image and dressed in elaborate Victorian fashion, Sophie's critical acclaim grew tenfold the following year, in 2010, when several images of her were prominently placed throughout Johannesburg's cityscape as part of a public art project for the Joburg City World Premier Annual Exhibition. Consisting of monumental billboards and building wraps, the images positioned South Africa's iconic Black maidservant as the preeminent welcoming sign for the swarms of international visitors drawn to South Africa for the FIFA World Cup. As one local passerby stated in response to the billboards, "It's welcoming me. I feel protected in the city" (Mail & Guardian, 2010). The images seemingly suggest a safe and sanitized South Africa where Black women, desirous of European ideals, dreamily engage the drudgery of domestic servitude to the benefit of the home front, the nation state, and the foreign other.

However, Sibande's project fits within a larger local history of domestic worker imagery. The deeper meaning and broader impact of her praxis become apparent through analysis of the wider contextual framework in which it exists. This lens reveals how Sibande is part and parcel of a dramatically new visual landscape of Black servitude in contemporary South African art. Indeed, Sophie reflects not only fresh style and content but also the Black empowerment ethos of the democratic order. She reflects the increasing propensity for Black women artists to access and disrupt the archive of apartheid imagery with alternative narratives. Sophie is a chief marker of a major generational shift from the representation of Black female laborers as static and disempowered to dynamic and assertive. Sophie is a marker or a kindred spirt of sorts to the many domestic worker effigies of her generation, among them Zanele Muholi's *Massa and Mina(h)* (2008), Marika Williams' *Miss Nothing* (2008–2009), Senzeni Marasela's *Theodora Comes to Jo'Burg Series* (2003–present), and Thembi Mtshali's *Woman in Waiting* (2001). Ranging from photography to performance to multimedia, Black women are inserting themselves into visual historiographies of domesticity and creating them anew.

What accounts for the recent proliferation of Black domestic worker images in South African art? What is the impulse behind and the basis for suddenly rendering the invisible visible? Why is it that Black women artists are particularly keen to embody and deploy the domestic worker trope as a means of critical articulation? Are these embodiments and representations propagated or circumscribed by the problems of patronage, public sensibility, press, and political demand that govern creative production, especially for people of color? Are Black women artists motivated to access the archives of apartheid imagery, to add new labels and addendums to the materials housed there, out of a sense of obligation? Are Black women artists, in other words, responsible for carrying, voicing, and visualizing the hardships of those who once could not and those who still cannot utter their own truths? What can the Black female imagination reveal about Black realities today? Moreover, what added meaning do we derive from Sibande who is the only artist of her generation to disrupt dominant images of Black domestics by incorporating life-size Black mannequins as critical devices in her work?

South African-based artist and critic Marion Arnold is among the first to raise and attempt answers to questions about the prevalence of Black women domestic workers in South African art. Looking particularly at Thomas Baines' 1873 pictorial image, "Craddock Place, Port Elizabeth," Dorothy Kay's 1956 portrait, "Cookie, Annie Mavata," Keith Dietrich's 1985 photo-realist image, "Mmopeng, Mmamule, and Mmathabeng," and Irma Stern's 1995 painting, "Maid in Uniform," Arnold exposes how White South African artists, male and female, place themselves in and understand themselves through the Black female domestic worker image. Her research reveals a century-long genealogy of White South African artistry in which Black female domestic workers serve as proxies capturing and projecting affirmations of privilege back onto the White self. In 1996, two years after the democratic election, Arnold argued that South Africa's most problematic images are its portrayals of domestic workers. Twenty-five years since the rise of democracy and Arnold's initial research, the domestic worker trope continues to labor as a vehicle for White fantasies about Black female identity. Recent applications of the trope appear in works by Penny Siopis, Jane Alexander, Gisele Wulfsohn, Peter Weinberg, Rose Shakinovsky, Roger Ballen, Steven Cohen, Coral Spencer, Lenora Van Staden, Alice Mann, and Brett Michael Inness, among several others.

Beezy Bailey is arguably the most audacious of these. Heir to one of South Africa's wealthiest White families, Bailey sculpts, paints, and performs provocative artworks that often challenge racial divides. He excited controversy when he submitted four linocuts to the 1991 Cape Town Triennial, one of which was entered under his own name and promptly rejected. However, for his other submissions, Bailey disguised himself as Joyce Ntobe, a fictitious Black domestic worker whom he later adopted as his alter ego. The Ntobe works were widely celebrated. One of them, entitled, "Go Home," which represents the treacherously long and congested journey that Black laborers embarked upon to navigate apartheid cities, was promptly purchased by the South African National Gallery.

Bailey's Ntobe prints strategically deploy a low cost and relatively simple printmaking technique that Black South African artists at Rorke's Drift mastered and popularized in the 1960s to critique their lived experiences. The black and white etchings depict urban life, the built environment, and religious references. However, in a slight turn away from the Rorke's Drift artists, the Ntobe pieces also portray arrant images of Black female servitude. For example, *Washing Up* shows a silent, diminutive domestic worker that seamlessly blends into the kitchen scenery surrounding her. Positioned slightly off-center, with her back to the viewer and faceless, her bodily form conforms to the vertical lines framing the stove, the laundry machine, the sink cabinet, the well-polished floor, and the garbage can – such that the viewer might well look past her to the open landscape from which she is shut off. In effect, Bailey appropriates Black identity and visual language to realize his creative career.

Bailey's stunt reveals much about how contemporary Black South African art has historically entered the mainstream, and perhaps also both how much and how little has changed since the 1990s. Black artworks are commonly typecast, interpreted and valued on the basis of their ability to project familiar narratives of Black struggle in readily identifiable ways. Process and technique are certainly a part of the equation, but these are generally seconded to revealing content. The domestic worker figure is particularly salient in this regard because it channels longstanding and continuous codes of racial hierarchy that cross between past and present, public and private, White and Black lives. As Sibande aptly puts it in connection with her own domestic worker alter ego, "If Sophie is not your mother, she is your auntie. If she is not your auntie, she's your neighbor. If she's not your neighbor, she's the woman who cleans for you. So we all relate to her. She's every woman"(BBC News, 2016). Indeed, as South African poet and women studies scholar Gabeba Baderoon points out, domestic service is synonymous with Black femaleness in South African civil society and it defines how Black women enter and occupy the public sphere (Baderoon, 2014). Conceived in colonialism and anchored in the apartheid experience, the Black woman domestic worker trope is now a de facto lieu du memoire, a site of memory in its own right, emerged from the bowels of backrooms, toilet sheds, and the tucked away corners of rooftop attics to become hypervisible in the art mainstream.

As neither a prop nor a backdrop, Sophie constitutes a strategic intervention in the corpus of Black domestic worker imagery in South African contemporary art. Instead of working in service to the White ego, Sophie stands in a formidable show of Black female agency and self-actualization. She embodies and projects resistance to dominant constructions of Black womanhood. In and through her creation of Sophie, Sibande reclaims, refashions, and revisions Black domestic workers in ways that, as Black feminist scholar bell hooks puts it, "white folk and black men could not even begin to understand"(hooks, 1992, 120). In effect, through Sophie, Sibande restores autonomy, dignity, and integrity to being habitually tortured with degradation, injustice, and erasure.

## The limits of dominant discourse in imagining Black womanhood

Dominant scholarship has long struggled with recognizing the beauty and complexity of Black womanhood. For example, in her seminal essay, "Why Have There Been No Great Women Artists," American feminist and art historian Linda Nochlin writes, "Using as a vantage point of their situation as underdogs in the realm of grandeur, and outsiders in the realm of ideology, women can reveal institutional and intellectual weaknesses in general, and . . . take part in the creation of institutions in which clear thought – and true greatness – are challenges open to anyone" (Nochlin, 76). "Disadvantage," she writes, "may indeed be an excuse; it is not, however, an intellectual position" (Nochlin, 76). For Nochlin, establishing space and equal footing for women artists generally means renegade bootstrapping. It means exposing, redressing, and healing the gaping wounds of gender inequity in the annals of art history. Countering patriarchy is the raison d'etre, the rallying call for women of all walks of life to band together under the broad rubric of womanhood. Hard-lined and homogenizing, Nochlin's words reflect the tenor of dominant feminist rhetoric. Moreover, her sentiments mark a pivotal turn in feminist discourse, but mostly for those who are White, privileged, and in many ways protected by the very patriarchies they seek to disrupt – women who are largely detached from the socio-cultural realities of the rest of the world, who, in their stalwart efforts to dismantle patriarchal authority inadvertently advance a parallel hegemonic critical paradigm of their own. In her response to Nochlin's essay, art historian Frida High Tesfagiorgis pinpoints how problematic underlying assumptions and ideologies frame dominant discussions and work to the detriment of underrepresented communities. She argues that Black women artists translate and deploy their experiences into unique aesthetics encoded with styles, morals, themes, forms, and subjects that are both specific to their realities and resistant to Eurocentric norms. The problem is that these acts of creative resistance are commonly misunderstood or completely overlooked by dominant discourses because they encompass unconventional visual strategies and priorities. In other words, dominant scholarship cannot identify or understand the complexity of Black women's creative practice.

Here, Michael Eric Dyson's description of White blindness to Black life is apropos. He writes to White audiences,

> At birth, you are given a pair of binoculars that see black life from a distance, never with the texture of intimacy. Those binoculars are privilege; they are status, regardless of your class. . . . Those binoculars are also stories, bad stories, biased stories, harmful stories, about how black people . . . can't be helped by . . . even God himself. These beliefs don't make it into contemporary books, or into most classrooms. But they are passed down, informally, from one white mind to the next.
>
> (Dyson, 2016)

"Whiteness is blindness," Dyson concludes (Dyson, 2016). "It is the wish not to see what it will not know" (Dyson, 2016). Consequently, Black women are either looked at and not seen or completely looked over. At the same time, societal demands pressure Black women to turn a blind eye to the bitter realities of inequity plaguing their world, to naively embrace the status quo, and to discard themselves in service to others who share but also sustain aspects of their oppression. On this basis, Tesfagiorgis advocates for and advances a critical Black feminist discourse, without which, she argues, "Black women artists and their production will remain behind the veils of art history" (Tesfagiorgis, 2001).

Though Tesfagioris made the call for a critical discourse that centers Black women some forty years ago, there remains an urgent need to carry out this important work. Studies of Sibande's artistry overwhelmingly concentrate on European attributes in her costume dresses, mostly dismissing or suggesting only in passing that the deliberately blackened skin of her mannequin figures also articulate profound meaning. For example, following her main arguments that Sibande's artworks are otherworldly, magical, and dwarfing, curator Amanda Krugliak notes that the artist "intentionally exaggerates the painted blackness of the mannequin, referencing the daunting gravity of cultural heritage and how it inevitably continues to define identity regardless of one's awareness, resilience, or resolve" (Krugliak, 2019). Krugliak references Sibande's racialization of Sophie as a cursory afterthought and evades the broader implications of the artist's intentionality. Her reading guides viewers to closely examine Sophie's size and the extravagant yardage, pleats, and folds of her skirt but stops short of critically interrogating whether and how Sophie's black skin implies alternative ways of Black female being that are not necessarily preoccupied with the weight of race as a definitive social condition from which there may be desire yet no effective means of escape.

In turn, visual and applied arts scholars Anne Scheffer, Ingrid Stevens, and Amanda du Preez argue that Sibande is neither critical nor provocative in her representation of the Black female body but instead deploys mimicry to support patriarchal representations of femininity. For them, Sibande's mannequins perpetuate and fortify Western norms. They argue, "Sophie generally seems to comply with patriarchal ideals . . . [she] is represented as a mannequin, which inherently presents an ideal physical form for women to aspire to (an ideal provided for women in the patriarchal paradigm)" (Scheffer, 2017, 18). Dismissing Sibande's mannequins as mimicry without inherent meaning undermines both the artistic motivation to contextualize the work and the capacity of mannequins to function as multifaceted signifiers. The broader symbolic meaning and implications of black mannequins in contemporary art and, more specifically, in Sibande's creative practice are largely overlooked.

Critics of Sibande's work seem to readily draw upon historical conceptions of mannequins as museological, artistic, and commercial tools strictly employed for and animated by fashion display. Scholarship on the subject ranges from consideration of how mannequin functions have evolved over time, beginning with their earliest documented use in European history as naturalistic wooden forms in fifteenth century Italian sculpture and painting, shifting to their increasing popularity throughout the eighteenth and nineteenth centuries in Paris, France (Munro, 2014, 31–33). Other work examines how mannequins and associated surrogate figures like dolls, puppets, models, and marionets reflect the nexus of postmodern dreams, realities, and tensions of human identity, culture, and ideology into the twentieth and twenty-first centuries (Munro, 2014, 31–33). Dominant discourses in art, fashion, and costume history offer remarkable insight on the history and functionality of mannequins over time, but they do so almost exclusively within the narrow confines of Eurocentrism. Critics of Sibande's work replicate this interpretive approach and, in so doing, overlook how black mannequins overlap, intersect with, and split from master narratives to produce alternative applications of human lay figures.

However, literary scholar Sarah Nuttall moves beyond analysis of costume dress to consider how Sibande's mannequins invoke meaning through representative skin surface. For her, the mannequin's blackness is "intensifie[d] . . . into something not really nameable" (Nuttall, 2013, 427). Its shiny veneer is an impenetrable force field from which the weight and pain of past assaults slip free to afford new ways of knowing the black female body. Nuttall writes,

> Sibande's 'sealed' figures . . . move away from the language of wounds and flesh, and begin to explore one of cladding and sealedness, with a particular interest in surfaces made . . . "so shiny as to blur and challenge the distinction between raced human skin and the more self-consciously plastic dimension of the mannequin figure."
>
> (ibid., 428)

In other words, Nuttall reads Sibande's richly varnished black mannequins as a cross between unnatural and futuristic. She discounts the historical force and contemporary relevance of their blackness to suggest their performance as avatars surpassing instead of explicating issues of race and gender in the present tenor of our time. Impenetrability is surely part and parcel of Sibande's artistic intent but the implication that her creative strategy involves glossing over Blackness is problematic. So too is the assertion that Blackness is incomprehensible. Here, it seems that Sophie is disrobed of Victorian regalia and re-assigned an ill-fitting and hyper-transgressive costume of post-racial sensibility.

Existing studies demonstrate habitual tendencies to evade rather than embrace Sophie's Blackness as a crucial defining feature. These tendencies shape intellectual discourse, but they also inform display strategies, object labels, and interpretive programming in museum settings, which can, in turn, contribute to skewed public perceptions of meaning and value. The decision whether to direct attention to Sophie's elaborate dress or to the attributes of her skin is largely the prerogative of curatorial vision – and so much can be lost when intellectual authority lacks desire or capacity to see and engage Blackness in all its richness and complexity.

The label for *Sophie-Merica* at the Smithsonian Institution's National Museum of African Art, for example, reads, "Beneath [Sophie's] skirt bursts a Cinderella-like gown to reveal the indomitable imagination of a woman otherwise defined by domestic toil" (*Sophie-Merica* Object Label). However, defining Sophie by her employ is a reductive strategy that homogenizes Black womanhood into a single image of servitude. Subjecting her imaginative power to the confines of a Cinderella fairytale diminishes her deliberately blackened skin into a shallow casing for illusions of grandeur. The label leaves Sophie's black skin as an unaddressed visual marker and, as such, replicates the habit of erasure that Sibande deliberately confronts. Moreover, the label not only cues but also inadvertently reinforces longstanding misperceptions of Black inferiority. Whereas museums can conceivably facilitate understanding and foster community, diverse perspectives and broad cultural competencies are critical to pushing past problematic legacies of stereotyping and misinterpretation.

South African photographer and Sibande contemporary Zanele Muholi captures the essence of the dilemma through an alternative lens in her 2004 photograph, *What Don't You See When You Look at Me*. The image depicts a scarred black-skinned forearm alongside a midriff covered with a white top, black belt, and gray bottom. Everything in the image is off-center and nothing appears in its entirety. Consequently, the subject of the shot is uncertain. It is uncertain whether the image depicts a male, female, or non-binary subject, whether the forearm belongs to the body, whether the body is whole or disfigured, alive or dead, or standing or reclining. It is also unclear whether the hand to the forearm is pocketed or exposed, whether the bottoms are pants or a skirt, whether the body is real or plastic. These defining attributes are each a matter of perspective, perspective which is necessarily subjective and incomplete. The viewer cannot know what it cannot see but remains, nonetheless, prone to reaching conclusions. The power of the image, therefore, emerges from what is shown as much as it does from all that is out of view. Yet, in and through flagging the subject's black skin with a gaping pink flesh wound, Muholi manages to convey provocative messaging about impenetrability and interiority, about the ineffectiveness of sight as a definitive explanatory tool, and about the significance of peeling back layers and, quite literally, cutting deeper into surface skin to access alternative possibilities of being and belonging.

The title of the photograph, *What Don't You See When You Look at Me*, is as provocative as the image itself. It not only challenges viewers to confront their assumptions but also to examine the image from an alternative angle that privileges recognition of the unknown instead of perceived expertise as a starting place for understanding. It exposes the impossibility of knowing it all as it offers opportunities to probe the self and the other in equal measure. The image captures and reflects the rhetorical qualities of its title, and the title provides a plain answer to the question it posits – which is, you don't know what you don't see you when you look at me, because you can't.

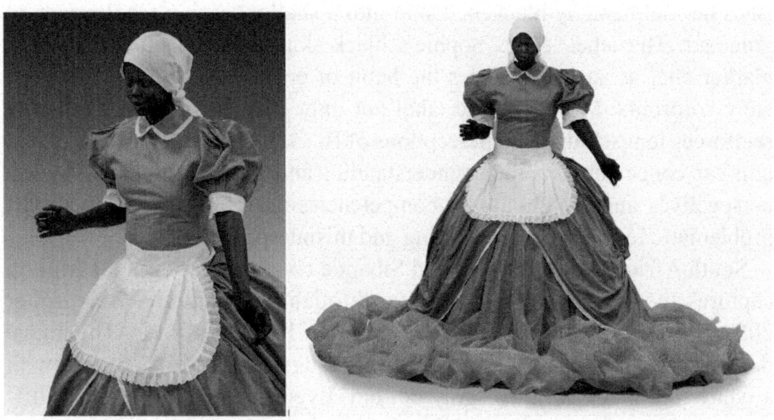

*Figure 7.1* Mary Sibande. *Sophie-Merica*. 2009.

*Source:* National Museum of African Art, Smithsonian Institution, Washington, DC.

Sibande exudes a similar ethos. She confronts the challenges of bias and skewed vision by sealing Sophie's eyes shut (Figure 7.1). She does not look outward for validation, definitions of being, or engagement of any kind but instead locates and affirms herself from within herself. Sophie's shut eyes suggest a conscious choice to block out the world around her in effort to realize different possibilities. Sibande shares,

> Sophie's most powerful gift is her ability to dream. She goes to work wearing a maid's uniform. But then she closes her eyes and starts to imagine things. . . . [H]er dreams become a reality for her and visible to us.
>
> (Sibande, 2013)

In effect, Sibande privileges internal reflection over spectator sport. She not only constructs Sophie such that she projects alternative Black female imagery, but she also shields Sophie from witnessing and absorbing the negative looks that are thrust upon her.

Moreover, Sibande deliberately fashions Sophie in the same armor worn by Black women who have policed their words and bodies in response to unjust societal conditions for time immemorial. Sophie "sees no evil, speaks no evil, hears no evil." Her face communicates alternative Black female experiences, sensibilities, and notions of socio-cultural integration. It signifies the complicated ways that Black female identity is experienced, constructed, represented, and understood. Her carefully sculpted, smooth, polished black skin and closed eyes suggest silence and impenetrability, which, in Black feminist discourse, are a show of power. To evoke Toni Morrison's powerful speech art, the Black female body is a formidable site of memory that articulates its continuous endurance of "unspeakable things" in "unspoken" ways (Morrison, 1994, 168–169).

The poetry of African American bard and civil rights activist Dr. Maya Angelou is particularly illuminating here. In her poem, *The Mask*, written in honor of a maid that she studied for nine months, Angelou reveals how Black womanhood exists between two modes of being: survival and submission. The poem describes how the maid robotically laughs the same pitiful laugh at each juncture on her journey between the house that she cleans each day and the home she returns to each night.

Following her public recital of *The Mask* at the Lewisham Hippodrome in 1987, Angelou explains that a studious observer knows that the maid's mechanical laugh, in fact, is not a laugh at all but instead a hollow open mouth gesture coupled with a monotonous, dispassionate repetition of sound to cue acknowledgment. The laugh is a double-sided shield that projects submission to the outer world while guarding access to the Black woman's private world of authentic, yet unsafe, thoughts and desires. Submission, in this respect, is an unwritten power code that works in defense of Black womanhood.

Dr. Angelou's timeless words resonate with the poignant title-question posed in Zanele Muholi's 2004 work, *What Don't You See When You Look at Me*, the answer to which, for Black women, is seemingly, perpetually, always, already NOTHING. But the magic in Sibande's exhibition, *Long Live the Dead Queen*, is that it pushes the alternative vision of Black femaleness even when and where there is an inability or plain refusal to acknowledge its presence. Sibande challenges spectators to learn to recognize and read the stories told in and through the silences and impenetrable spaces constructed in defense of black being and belonging. Indeed, Sophie's body functions as a hermeneutic through which Black female autonomy is summarily restored.

In this context, Sibande uses the mannequin figure to disrupt and redirect the power dynamics of seeing and being seen such that it is not the Black domestic maidservant, Sophie, that is invisible but instead all who peer upon her and are not seen back. In lieu of a counter gaze, Sophie's black skin functions as a dynamic site of engagement. It is a critical threshold between Black interior and exterior worlds upon which Sibande inscribes complex meaning by pulling aspects of each into the other. Interestingly, though her eyes are shut, Sophie's shiny black skin performs as a reflective surface that enables gazers to witness themselves in the act of watching and reading Black womanhood. Consequently, when viewers see Sophie, they also see themselves, their assumptions, and their ways of being. The question is whether viewers can locate themselves as subjects and resolve flaws in their seeing habits.

## Assertion through insertion: autobiographical Sophie

A girl-child of the interregnum and a mother of the born-free generation, Sibande, who was born in Mpumalanga in 1982 and raised in Johannesburg, where she received advanced degrees in fine art, deploys myriad strategies to insert herself within the problematic conditions of Black servitude to negotiate, interrogate, and subvert gendered and racialized subjectivities in South African civil society. Coming of age during the interregnum meant not only surviving between two social orders but also between two identities, "one known and discarded, the other unknown and undetermined" (Gordimer, 2019). Indeed, as Nobel laureate Nadine Gordimer eloquently puts it, the resolution of these complex, troubled South African identities, Black and White, necessarily depends upon finding a way out of the perpetual clutter and imagery of master-servant relationships. Accordingly, Sibande enters South African art history with the possession, authority, and consciousness of a personal experience steeped in a precarious state of in-betweenness, of being and becoming, of constantly transforming. These complexities shape and inform her construction of Sophie.

Consequently, Sibande is at the forefront of depicting new images of Black domestic servitude in South Africa. Her creative oeuvre is informed by and firmly rooted both within the context of her personal lineage and societal conditions. *Long Live the Dead Queen* debuts four iterations of Sophie, each one simultaneously representing multiple experiences of Black womanhood. Each mannequin is cast in the artist's personal image and carries both an individualized name and the generic domestic worker moniker, Sophie, as a symbolic reference and socio-cultural connection to the plethora of Black domestics throughout the country. Although the names and costumes expand in size and meaning with each new creation, Sibande consistently injects the surface layers of her mannequins with figurative genetic memory and connective skin tissue that link realities of Black womanhood across time and space. Sibande shares,

> I started [Sophie] as a celebration of the women in my family, who were all maids – from my great-grandmother up to my mother. I was born in the 80s, so I had a different upbringing and a very different life compared to generations of South African women before me: I'm the first woman in my family who attended university. The issue of servitude within this family has been passed on from one generation to the next – until I came along. I try to bring in new perspectives as an artist, since I will never be a maid, yet can dress like and perform as one. In this role I continue in a line of very strong women. By trying to capture some of their experiences, Sophie was created to be the next in line.
>
> (Wellerhaus, 2013)

The first in the familial chain is Sophie-Elsie, a representation of Sibande's great grandmother. Sophie-Merica and Sophie-Velucia depict Sibande's grandmother and mother, respectively. The last act, Sophie-Ntombikaysie portrays Sibande herself. Through deliberate construction of myriad Black female identities, Sibande strategically inserts herself not simply into the lineage of Black servitude from which she stems, and ultimately surpasses, but also into persistent continuities of domesticity in South Africa today. Sibande's strategic act of insertion enlivens and adds depth of meaning to the mannequin figures in her work.

Salah Hassan's conceptualization of insertion is a particularly instructive lens through which to view Sibande's mannequins. He describes insertion as a creative technique that African women artists commonly deploy to interrogate and disrupt misrepresentations of their image in dominant discourse. It relies upon deliberate manipulation of self-imagery and negotiation of complex subject positions located both within and beyond the mainstream. The technique traffics in the postcolonial urge to dissect and then redo that which has already been attempted in order to codify, to counter, or to correct the original and/or to map and give voice to alternatives. Hassan defines insertion as ambiguous and multi-layered, referencing both "the sexual metaphor or pun, often as associated with the act of insertion" and an "act of counter-penetration, an assertion of one's own subjectivity in response to objectification" (Hassan, 2002). Insertion might also involve "verisimilitude," which Hassan describes, in this context, as a cross between "reflection and projection," based on the artist's urge to engage dominant perceptions and their underlying assumptions.

Through this lens, Sibande's personified mannequins emerge as recuperative sites where histories and recurring themes of Black family rupture are rewritten. Under apartheid's restrictive control policies, Black mothers serving as domestic workers were routinely separated from their children for extended periods owing to job expectations and challenges of navigating segregated city spaces. In fact, domestic service was exceptionally demanding work during the apartheid years, requiring between sixty-one and eighty-four hours weekly and even more time for live-in maids who only received time-off for holidays (Cock, 1994). As writer Sindiwe Magona shares, personal family time between Black mothers and their natural born children was both "a luxury and a privilege" (Magona, 1990, 124). The travesty was not just that Black mothers and their children suffered little time together but that Black mothers were made responsible for raising privileged White children largely at the expense of their own. These broken familial bonds become sutured back together and superimposed atop Sophie's skin when Sibande inserts and intertwines herself within the subject positions of her great-grandmother, grandmother, and mother. The insertion asserts a stream of Black existential circumstance not lost to Sibande but instead made part and parcel of the essence of her being.

While domestic toil under apartheid undoubtedly involved extreme hardship, Sibande is concerned with pushing past the pain to locate and place within her artistry the positive realities born of the experience. She recalls how as a child her grandmother told her stories laced with aspirational hope.

> Sophie's stories are intrinsically linked to what the women in my family told me when I was young, but they also go beyond this. Most of my grandmother's stories were about aspiration. I assumed similar circumstances for Sophie but wanted to make sure that she went further and actually gained what she wished for.
>
> (Wellershaus, 2013)

Sibande pulls from the memory banks of her youth to envision herself, as a celebrated, formally trained artist and not a maid, the full manifestation of her grandmother's dreams.

Perhaps this is why Sophie's face is Sibande's face, and also why the face never changes. No matter the hyphenated name of the subject piece, -Ntombikayisie, -Merica, -Elsie, or -Velucia, the dream and reality of familial progress is represented in and through the artist's mirror image.

It is noteworthy that the pieces comprising *Long Live the Dead Queen* exist in clear contradistinction to works like Claudette Schreuders' *The Family Tree*, which includes a series of wooden sculptures and prints modeled on photographs from the artist's family album. One piece, entitled *Mother and Child* (Figure 7.2), is a representation of the lone Black face resident in Shreuders' archive. The piece depicts a Black maid and White child. The maidservant's eyes hold an open blank stare. Her mouth is slightly agape. Her feet are firmly rooted as her arms cradle the active child in her care. Her surface skin reveals the imperfections and circular patterning of the cypress woodgrain from which she is cut, suggesting a repetitive cycle of life that is mirrored in the maid/madam relationship. The coddled White child will grow to become the maid's madam, the maid will produce children of her own who will follow in her steps and serve other White masters, and the cycle will continue for generations. Unlike Sibande's mannequins, Schreuders' figure is a static personification of the servicing and serviceable Black woman. The maidservant is reduced to and weighted down with superimposed responsibilities of motherhood. As evidenced by the baby she pampers and her otherwise flat disposition, the future relies upon her sacrifice, her capacity to employ every bit of herself in service to a world in which she has no agency and no identity other than workhorse. She is, at best, a surrogate whose identity and purpose are fused to servitude to an empowered white other. Consequently, *Mother and Child* perpetuates racial norms as it portrays anxieties of being and belonging, allegories of familial rupture, and the ironies of motherhood in a nation fraught with racial tension and lopsided labor and employment practices. Furthermore, its visual signifiers propagate the spectacle and falsity of Black female inferiority.

In contrast, Sibande's *Sophie* (Figure 7.1) is unbothered, unburdened, and unbossed.

She is defined neither by accompanying children nor tools of toil. Her eyes are closed and, as such, neither receive, reject, embrace nor return the colonial gaze. Her feet are unexposed, but her arms and fingering hands imply active motion just as her open mouth implies capacity to inhale. *Sophie is* self-absorbed and self-empowered. She is not in service to the state, the madam or a man but exists with herself, through herself, for herself. This becomes particularly evident in works like *Wish You Were Here*,

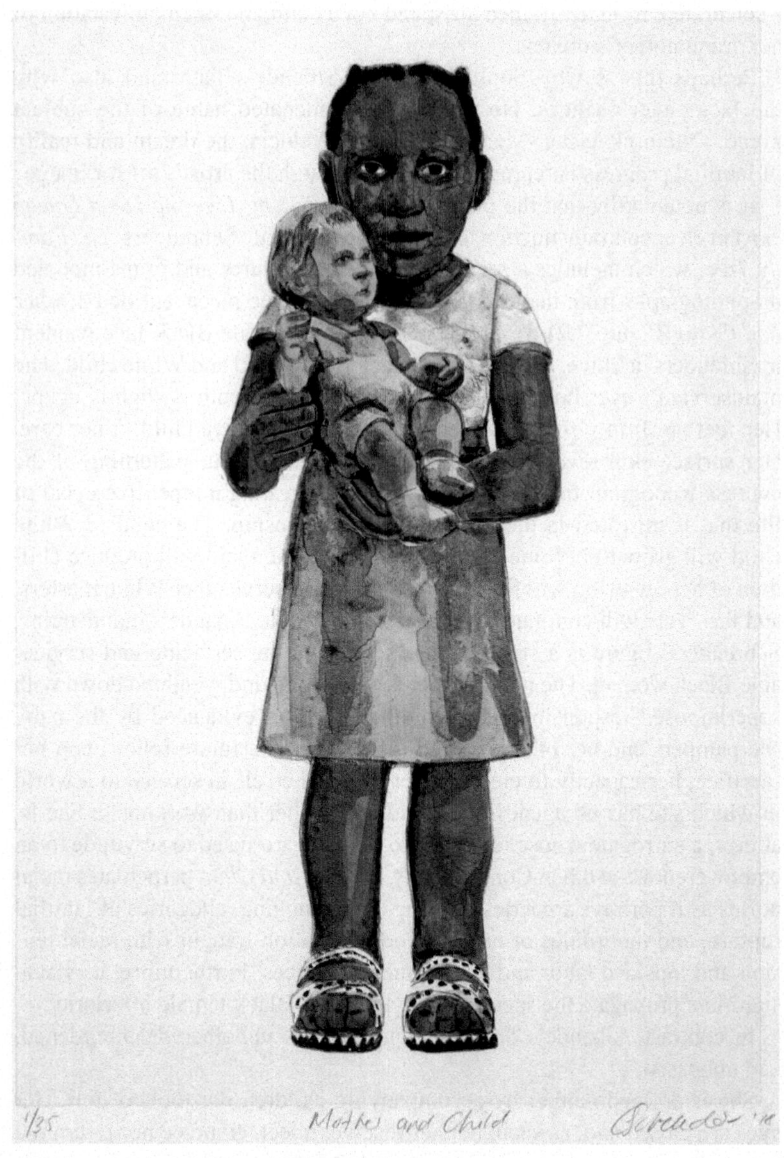


*Figure 7.2* Claudette Schreuders. *Mother and Child*. 1994.

*Source:* Courtesy of Stevenson, Cape Town and Johannesburg.

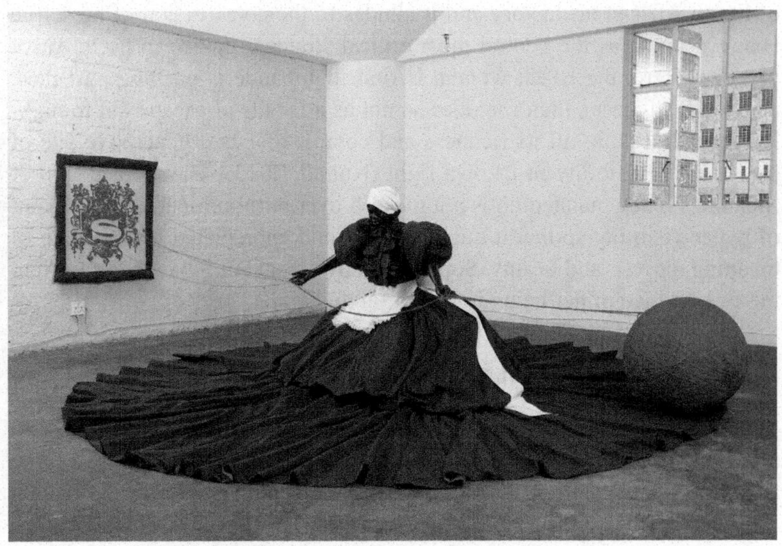

*Figure 7.3* Mary Sibande. *Wish You Were Here*, 2010.

*Source:* Image courtesy of the artist.

2010 (Figure 7.3), which captures Sophie fixated on inscribing a supersized version of her initial onto a wall hanging for all to see. In an interview with freelance artist Jessica Foli, Sibande suggests that the letter "S" might stand for "Super-Sophie or simply Sophie" (Foli, 2013, 373). Sophie is clearly preoccupied and self-centered. She is neither hyperactive nor burdened with babies, brooms, or balanced workloads on her head. If she is weighted down at all, then it is by the impossible dress that she wears which forbids her ability to perform as a workhorse. Consequently, Sophie defies reliance upon or preoccupation with the White other to instead retreat within herself where processes of self-discovery and self-recovery occur at her own volition. In effect, intimacies of domesticity are expanded from self and other to include the self in relation to the self. Sibande broadens the notion of insertion as an artistic technique by shifting her focus inward.

Sibande's creative practice works against reactionary efforts to redress the apartheid past that stripped Black women of dignity and self-acceptance. Hers is an artistry of initiation instead of response that establishes Black femininity as a self-possessed and generative site of engagement. In this context, insertion takes on added meaning that has little to do with sex, subjugation, or authenticity as Hassan's conceptual framework outlines. Here, insertion references how domestic workers entered and coped with their profession. It references how Sibande engages the imbalanced canon of South African art history and it alludes to the construction of herself, a Black woman, as the central most critical strategic device in her creative practice. Here, the Black woman is first. If Sibande is pushing past race, as Nuttall suggests, then she does so not as a means of escape but to highlight Blackness, in all its richness and complexity, as a generative site of power and possibility in its own right (Nuttall, 2013). The surface skin of Sibande's black mannequin is not glossed over but illuminated to the point of hyper-visibility so that it might be seen and appreciated for its depth of meaning, power, and beauty. Sophie, and by extension Sibande, grows into the full essence of her being in and through the blackness of her skin.

## Conclusion: Sophie's skin cells and scar tissue

Mannequins enable acknowledgement of the past, embrace of the present, and excitement about the future. Mary Sibande strategically deploys these attributes in her creations of Sophie. Her approach invites new ways of seeing Black female subjects in contemporary art that fit within a larger history of representation but also move in different directions. Although most of the scholarship on her work generally overlooks the deeper meaning of her mannequin figures, Sibande's work invites fresh critical perspectives that expand the boundary conditions of dominant intellectual discourse by placing black skin and Black women center focus.

Sibande personalizes her work through strategic acts of insertion that encourage learning from the past rather than evading or anxiously covering it up. The work also suggests that healing and progress will happen from the inside out for White and Black artist and critics alike.

## Works cited

Baderoon, Gabeba. "The Ghost in the House: Women, Race, and Domesticity in South Africa." *Cambridge Journal of Postcolonial Literary Inquiry* 1, no. 2 (2014): 173–188. https://doi.org/10.1017/pli.2014.17

Cock, Jacklyn. *Maids and Madams: Domestic Workers under Apartheid*. London: The Women's Press, Ltd, 1994.

Dyson, Michael Eric. "Death in Black and White." *The New York Times*, July 8, 2016. <www.nytimes.com/2016/07/10/opinion/sunday/what-white-america-fails-to-see.html>

Foli, Jessica. "Socio-Cultural Aspects of Clothing: The Resurrection of an Imagined Reality in Mary Sibande's *Long Live the Dead Queen*." Essay. In *Africa and Beyond: Arts and Sustainable Development*, edited by J. Patrick Ebewo, Ingrid Stevens, and Mzo Sirayi, 373. Newcastle, UK: Cambridge Scholars Publishing, 2013.

Gordimer, Nadine. "Living in the Interregnum." *The New York Review of Books*. Accessed November 12, 2019. <www.nybooks.com/articles/1983/01/20/living-in-the-interregnum/>

Hassan, Salah. "Insertions: Self and Other in Contemporary African Art." In *Authentic/Ex-Centric: Conceptualism in Contemporary African Art*, edited by Annie E. Coombes, Rory Doepel, et al., 26–49. Venice: Forum for African Arts, 2002.

hooks, bell. *Black Looks: Race and Representation*, 120. Boston, MA: South End Press, 1992.

Krugliak, Amanda. "Sibande on Campus: U-M LSA Institute for the Humanities." *LSA*. Accessed December 17, 2019. <https://lsa.umich.edu/humanities/gallery/sibande-on-campus.html>

Magona, Sindiwe. *To My Children's Children*, 124. Cape Town, 1990.

Morrison, Toni. "Unspeakable Things Unspoken." *Within the Circle* (1994): 368–398. https://doi.org/10.2307/j.ctv1134fjj.33

Munro, Jane. *Silent Partners Artist and Mannequin from Function to Fetish*. New Haven, CT: Yale University Press, 2014.

Nochlin, Linda. "Why Have There Been No Great Women Artists?" *Women, Art, and Power and Other Essays* (2018): 145–178. https://doi.org/10.4324/9780429502996-7

Nuttall, Sarah. "Wound, Surface, Skin." *Cultural Studies* 27, no. 3 (2013): 418–437. https://doi.org/10.1080/09502386.2013.780228.

Scheffer, Anne, Ingrid Stevens, and Amanda Du Preez. "Hysterical Representation in the Art of Mary Sibande." *de arte* 52, no. 2–3 (2017): 4–28. https://doi.org/10.1080/00043389.2017.1332503

Sibande, Mary. "Sophie Is Not the Only Strong Woman Populating Our Art Scene at the Moment." Interview by Elisabeth Wellershaus, *Contemporary And*, June 24, 2013. <www.contempoaryand.com/magazines/sophieis-not-the-only-strong-woman-populating-our-art-scene-at-the-moment/>

"Sophie in Jo'Burg Skyline." *Mail & Guardian*, November 1, 2010. <www.youtube.com/watch?v=yAO5Nb9cHqQ>

"South African Artist Mary Sibande: 'Why I Want to Celebrate Maids'." *BBC News*, November 16, 2016. <www.bbc.com/news/world-africa-37935319>

Tesfagiorgis, Freida High W. "In Search of a Discourse and Critique/s That Center the Art of Black Women Artists." Essay. In *Black Feminist Cultural Criticism*, edited by Jacqueline Bobo, 148–172. Malden, MA: Blackwell, 2001.

Wellershaus, Elisabeth. "Sophie Is Not the Only Strong Woman Populating Our Art Scene at the Moment." *Contemporary And*, June 24, 2013. <www.contemporaryand.com/magazines/sophieis-not-the-only-strong-woman-populating-our-art-scene-at-the-moment/>

# Index

Note: Page numbers in *italics* indicate a figure on the corresponding page. Page numbers followed by "n" indicate a note.